MW01193455

How To Learn & Memorize French Vocabulary … Using A Memory Palace Specifically Designed For The French Language

Second Edition

Anthony Metivier, PhD

For language learners everywhere

Table of Contents

Acknowledgements iii

Why You Need To Read This Book iv

Overcoming The Main Obstacles To Memorization vii

Preface To The Second Edition x

PART ONE: BEFORE YOU BEGIN 1

Three Questions 2

Chapter 1: How The Magnetic Memory Method Began 4

Chapter 2: Memory Palace History 14

PART TWO: THE ART AND MECHANICS OF THE
MEMORY PALACE 19

Chapter 3: How To Build A Memory Palace 20

Chapter 4: Example Memory Palace 27

Chapter 5: Example Alphabet Memory Palace 50

PART THREE: FRENCH VOCABULARY MEMORY
PALACE CREATION 59

Chapter 6: Applying The Main Principles To Learning And
Memorizing French Vocabulary 60

Chapter 7: Notes On The Creation And Management Of Your
French Language Memory Palaces 72

Chapter 8: Example Memory Palace For the Letter A 76

Chapter 9: Example Memory Palace For The Letter C 82

Chapter 10: Example Memory Palace For The Letter F 86

Chapter 11: Choosing The Most Important Words, Building
Focus And Overcoming Procrastination For The Achievement
Of Fluency 90

PART FOUR: RETENTION AND RELAXATION 101

Chapter 12: How To Extend Memory Retention Using
Compounding Exercises & Generate Excitement For Learning
French Vocabulary 102

Chapter 13: How To Move French Vocabulary And Phrases Into Long-Term Memory Using The Simplest And Most Elegant Memory Technique In The World...............105

Chapter 14: How to Use Relaxation For French Vocabulary Memorization..110

PART FIVE: CONCLUSION..113

Chapter 15: Frequently Asked Questions 114

Chapter 16: This Magnetic Conclusion Is Just the Beginning 130

GLOSSARY AND BONUSES...144

Glossary..145

Further Resources For Memory & Language Learning Techniques 148

Secret Bonus #1...149

Secret Bonus #2 151

Secret Bonus #3 157

Spread The word!...168

Magnetic Memory Newsletter Volume 1.............................171

Magnetic Memory Newsletter Volume 2 172

Magnetic Memory Newsletter Volume 3 174

Magnetic Memory Newsletter Volume 4 175

Magnetic Memory Newsletter Volume 5 176

About The Author...177

Other Books By Dr. Anthony Metivier.................................179

Acknowledgements

Many people have been of invaluable assistance with the creation of this book and the development of the Magnetic Memory Method. My gratitude goes to Kathi McKinzie, Joshua Smith, Daniel Welsch, Jim Samuels, Michael Petri, Henry Schroeder, Alexander Berglin, David Mansaray, Luca Lampariello, Olly Richards, Roland Peters, Sergio Klein, Alberto Atalah, John Yeoman, Greg Taylor, Jonathan Levi, Steve Newman, Noel van Vliet, Natã Gomes, Gudrun Johnson-Stein, Kerry Russell, Stephan Si-Hwan Park, Tim Gerwing, Nils, Peiler, Theokritos Veskoukis, Haydee Windey, Sandra Vymetal and the thousands of readers and Magnetic Memory Method video course participants who have emailed me their questions, comments, support and invaluable feedback.

Why You Need To Read This Book

Have you ever said to yourself, "I have a bad memory"? Have you used that as an excuse for the poor progress you've made with learning French?

If so, I completely sympathize. In the past, my favorite saying when facing any type of memorization project (vocabulary, grammar, poems, scripts, math, music, etc.) was "I have a poor memory!" In fact, I have silently sworn so vehemently about my "bad memory" that, had I spoken my frustration out loud, my teachers would have kicked me out of class. Such was my frustration with memorizing.

My frustration increased until I finally created the unique Magnetic Memory Method utilizing the Memory Palace techniques taught in this book. The Magnetic Memory Method is a set of techniques based around the French alphabet that will help you acquire countless French words at a rapid pace. Rather than struggling to remember what used to be one or two new words a day, you can now memorize dozens of words in less than an hour using my system.

> **Memory Palace**: The place you store your images and information. Usually based on a building or other structure, though not always.

Within a month of applying myself to French using the Magnetic Memory Method described in this book, I knew the meaning and the sound of over 260 words. Within three months, I could read poetry, literature and newspapers that in the past would have sent me screaming for the dictionary.

I am always pleased to help people with their desire to memorize the vocabulary of new languages. I regularly have people tell me that they have successfully memorized their first 100 words within an hour using the techniques I teach. Make no mistake: these techniques work. They work for me, they work for everyone who has read my books and they will

> People tell me that they have successfully memorized their first 100 words within an hour.

work for you.

If you want access to the magic that has helped so many people reach their fluency goals, then this second edition of **How To Learn & Memorize French Vocabulary** is for you. Whether you are an adult, teenager or someone working with young students, you will benefit from this book.

Everyone dreams of learning at least one new language, but so few of us ever do. Many learn a handful of words and phrases, but most struggle to learn enough vocabulary for a decent conversation. My "guerilla" memory tactics are very attractive to people, especially when they realize that they help achieve near-fluency in a short period of time.

What Others Are Saying

★★★★★ I thought at first this was another read it and forget it language book. Was I ever wrong. I read the book through, and then went back and began implementing Dr. Metivier's methods. And they truly work. As he states, it takes a few hours (1to 5 hours) to organize, but once this is done, it is all up to you, and your imagination. And unlike other self-help language learning methods, your learning does not stop with the purchase of this book, far from it. Dr. Metivier kindly will send newsletters, advice, practically all one would need to help with his methods. This concise little book is worth many times its selling price. Merci beaucoup, Dr. Metivier for a gem. – Rick Montana

★★★★★ I waited to write my review of this book until I'd had a chance to put Metivier's technique to the test—about 6 weeks after I read it. I sure am glad I found this book—not just for memorizing French words, but for everything I want to remember! Unlike so many books about memory tricks or memory palaces, Metivier actually explains, meticulously, just how to go about building memory palaces and filling them up with the French words (or words of any language that uses the Roman alphabet) you want to remember. He tells you what preparation steps are necessary, gives examples of the kind of vivid imagery you're going to use, and even suggests a schedule in which you devote one day a month to each of the 26 letters of the alphabet. I'm 58 years old, learning French with an aim to be reasonably fluent in a year: thanks to this technique, I feel confident I can do it. I'm memorizing around 100 words a day now, and it's fun, too! - Fiona Webster

★★★★★ I gave this book 5 stars. Although I bought it to learn French. It has given me more than just French. It is a memory system that I can apply to many other aspects of my life. It makes any subject as well as french interesting and fun. Highly recommended. Thanks Anthony. - Tassie

Overcoming The Main Obstacles To Memorization

There are three obstacles standing between you and memorizing massive amounts of French vocabulary quickly and easily.

The Belief That You Don't Need A Memorization Strategy For Learning French Vocabulary

Most language learners rely on rote learning. They listen to tapes that prompt them to repeat the same phrases over and over again in the hopes that the vocabulary will stick with them. Be honest. You have secretly hoped that by merely repeating a word or phrase over and over, you will retain it in your mind forever. I'm not saying that this approach doesn't work, nor am I saying that audio trainings that use repetition aren't worth your while. They most certainly are.

What I am saying, however, is that the fantasy of rote learning makes many people give up because it simply does not work very well without a dedicated memorization strategy. Use and implement the techniques described in this book and you will succeed in your goal of learning French vocabulary.

The Belief That You Can't Use Memorization Techniques

People often tell me that memorization techniques simply don't work for them. I always confidently respond by saying, "Yes they will." I provide a quick demonstration taught at the end of this book and discuss scholarly evidence that proves that we all have the ability to memorize successfully any amount of information we choose when we have the right strategies in place.

Richard C. Atkinson's study of the use of memory techniques for language learning conducted at Stanford University is one of countless studies. Humorously, Atkinson calls the pen and paper, which many use for rote learning, a "cheap memory device" that is virtually worthless. In comparison, there is great value in the memory techniques offered in this book.

Repeatedly writing the same word again and again is a very old technique from the time when teachers smacked their students' knuckles for misbehavior. Just as physical punishment rarely improved anyone's behavior for long, and I don't think that rote memorization is going to give you permanent access to the words you want to own for good.

In closing his study, Atkinson concluded that all language-learning classes include memorization techniques in their curriculum. The incredible leaps made by language learners when using memorization techniques are indisputable.

> The incredible leaps made by language learners when using memorization techniques are indisputable

The Belief That This Business Of Memorization Is Too Much Work

The memorization strategies you will find in this book take between 2-5 hours to set up. Once you've prepared the path through the Memory Palace for yourself, the effects of the training will be immediate. The steps are so easy and fun that you'll quickly realize what a waste of time rote learning is. As soon as you've understood the memorization principles taught in this book and applied the system, you will be learning and retaining new French words in a matter of seconds.

Let me make a suggestion to you before we begin: Believe in the power of your mind. I failed to believe in my mind for a very long time, but now I know how quickly the ability to memorize large numbers of words from any language will open the doors of the world for anyone who learns these skills.

What you're about to discover isn't just for simple vocabulary. Understanding another culture requires a sophisticated vocabulary and one that is not limited to phrases related to basic greetings and travel. Obviously, you can use the system taught in this book to learn and retain those phrases, but my goal for you is to be able to sit with a dictionary and walk away with 50-100 words lodged in your mind within an hour or less.

The best part is that with a language like French, you are getting access to not just one culture, but the cultures of multiple countries. French remains a language spoken all around the world. This means that those with an advanced French vocabulary can experience greater pleasure when traveling than they have ever dreamed possible. When it comes right down to it, isn't pleasure what life is all about?

With an advanced French vocabulary, you can travel to these countries and experience them with greater intensity than you ever could have dreamed. You'll talk with people you could never have met otherwise. You'll receive service reserved for people who exhibit the finesse of learned language skills of the host country. If you are in business, you will make deals with greater ease and efficiency, particularly if you apply what you learn in this book to memorize how French speakers use their language to persuade.

With the system taught in this book, you will be able to enjoy French television, radio, newspapers and magazines much more quickly than rote learning could ever provide. You will enjoy French theatre and movies and even understand paintings and other art produced by French culture at deeper levels because you'll enjoy the ability to read the language and understand the nuances specific to those art forms. You can and will do this. You will love adapting this system to your individual learning style and enjoy massive success as a result. Give me 2-5 hours of your time and I will give you the techniques and abilities you need to memorize all the French vocabulary you could ever want without end.

Preface To The Second Edition

Congratulations on picking up this book. You've made a wise decision, one that will take your language learning to the next level if you use the techniques you are about to learn. The best part is you're about to experience memory improvement that can help with all areas of your life.

However, you do have to *use* the Magnetic Memory Method to experience its positive effects.
Sadly, not everyone will. The question is...

Will you?

Since first introducing the Magnetic Memory Method to language learners, I've received many reactions. Hundreds and hundreds of emails have poured into my inbox, and I've received postcards and Skype calls of praise. People have sent 45-minute long recordings explaining their success for my podcast. Teachers have gone on to share the Magnetic Memory Method in their classrooms after learning about it. The response has been nothing short of amazing.

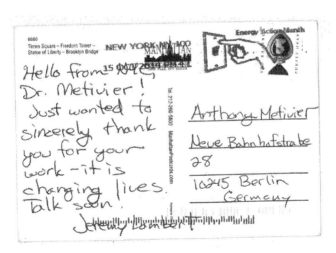

In addition, I've been pleasantly surprised to hear from people of all ages. I've spoken with parents of children as young as 6. Their children have built Memory Palaces and memorized stunning amounts of information. I've heard from senior citizens as old as 88 who have used the Magnetic Memory Method to perform absolute miracles of memory.

Age is *never* a factor for those who experience success with the memory techniques I teach. Language learners of all ages regularly report adding hundreds of words to their vocabulary in just a few days.

Yet at the same time, I've heard from people who haven't experienced these levels of success. All along, I've asked myself, "Why is this?" How is that so many people rocket to success with these techniques while others cannot penetrate them.

In preparing this second edition of *How To Learn & Memorize French Vocabulary*, I've kept this impasse in mind. Because I know that these techniques work, I feel an ethical duty to get them in the hands of as many language learners as possible. Not just any memory techniques, I'm talking about the techniques suited to the needs of particular people, the people who struggle with language learning to such a degree that they have given up.

> I know that these techniques work. I feel an ethical duty to get them in the hands of as many language learners as possible.

If there is a "magic bullet" for memorizing, retaining and recalling vocabulary, the Magnetic Memory Method is that elixir.

Why is this?

It's because languages cannot be learned if you cannot remember words. There's a lot of debate out there about how to best learn and memorize words, but until recently there have been few solutions, and the strategies that do work have the unfortunate effect of boring many people almost to death.

That's no exaggeration. If you've ever used one of those programs on your smart phone that shows you the digital equivalent of flash cards (spaced-repetition software), then you've probably felt the bite of that boredom. After all, you're pummeling your brain with a hammer, hoping that the words will stick. If you're not having fun with the method, then of course performance and outcome are going to suffer.

The Magnetic Memory Method solves the problem of boredom. It uses the natural powers of your imagination and things you already know and feel interested in as part of the learning process. If you wish, you can use the Magnetic Memory Method in conjunction with spaced-repetition software and index cards.

Therefore, if the first edition of this book has failed to help some readers, it can only be on the matter of fun for good reason. Much of what you're about to learn sounds on the surface like hard work. There are multiple steps to follow and it can feel like a long haul before you even get to learning and memorizing French vocabulary.

However, it really isn't a massive effort. We're talking about 2-5 hours to learn the Magnetic Memory Method and get some quick victories with it. After that, your jet is in the air and it is smooth flying thereafter, but you have to follow the steps. You need to do so with a spirit of inquiry and experimentation.

This book and the Magnetic Memory Method really aren't for people who can't bring those two qualities to the game, because it is a game, one with all the classic characteristics of challenge and triumph. It will keep you young and sharpen your memory while boosting your French vocabulary. It's only fun if you understand the rules of play and follow them. What fun would baseball or hockey be if people didn't know or follow its rules?

As in all sports, there are tiny little exceptions here and there, places to drift outside of the guidelines and innovate and that's where you need to be your own umpire or referee. You need to examine the playing field and make decisions based on the rules of play, but no one can break rules they don't understand, much less make informed decisions.

So if you're reluctant, doubtful or downright resistant, keep the spirit of play in mind. All I ask is that you open your mind and your memory of your past and your interests. Then I ask you to apply what you already know to learning vocabulary words that you don't know at this point.

When you can do that, the Magnetic Memory Method will help open the doors of fluency in ways you cannot yet imagine. Add it to your daily reading, writing, speaking and listening practice, and you will experience real magic. You'll find yourself recognizing words and phrases as you go along and be able to bring them almost effortlessly to your mouth. The more you practice, the easier and faster it gets. You won't know how you got along without this language learning technique.

The Magnetic Memory Method has worked miracles for thousands of people who brought their own spirit of play to the game. In this second edition, I've taken the feedback I've received to heart. I've injected what I've learned from my readers and students to make this a more useful book. For those who struggled to understand the Magnetic Memory Method, I have expanded the instructions. I've added illustrations to make the steps more visual. Since the first edition, I have interviewed many language learning and memory experts and can now share their wisdom and perspectives with you.

One final note before you get started. The wealth of information you're about to receive will serve you for life so please do read this book from cover to cover. Take notes and take action. I'm not really a big *Star Wars* fan, but I always think Yoda is worth quoting. "Do or do not. There is no try." When Luke Skywalker says he's doesn't believe it, Yoda says, "That is why you fail." As long as you follow the steps by taking full and complete action by building well-formed Memory Palaces and experimenting with the other elements of memorization you'll learn, you will succeed.

WAIT!

I have created Magnetic Memory Worksheets that go along with this book. Download site:

http://www.magneticmemorymethod.com/free-magnetic-memory-worksheets/

As a reader of this book, you'll also receive a *complimentary* subscription to the prestigious Magnetic Memory Newsletter – while it's still free. Subscribe now and get the only information that will keep your memory ***Magnetic*** for years to come.

PART ONE: BEFORE YOU BEGIN

Three Questions

Let me begin this book with a STRONG recommendation. Take a moment to answer the three quick questions below. You can easily email me your answers with "Memory Questions Answered" in the subject line for a free gift that will continue your education in the art of learning and memorizing.

That's it for now. You have lots to do and a very exciting adventure ahead of you! Make sure you subscribe to the Magnetic Memory Method newsletter and watch your email inbox for ongoing announcements, and make sure to get in touch with any questions you may have by email at <u>learnandmemorize@zoho.com</u>.

Three Questions That Can Make All The Difference In The World

Before you begin reading this book, you can jump-start your success by answering three important questions. People who take the time to reflect a little about what their memory means to them experience much greater success.

So to encourage you to take this step, I have a special free offer …

Send In Your Answers To These Three Questions For A Special Gift!

This exercise will only take a few minutes to complete and the gift you'll receive will take your language learning experience to a whole new level. Of course it's up to you if you want to partake in this part of the memory training, but if you're one of the rare few who is truly serious about improving your ability to learn and memorize French, all you have to do is email me your answers with "French Memory Questions Answered" in the subject line at learnandmemorize@zoho.com. Please include a copy of your receipt for this book to confirm your purchase.

Magnetic Memory Question #1:

What is your personal "Memory Myth" with respect to language learning? Memory myths include any programming you may have received as a young person or continue to receive in your daily life. This programming includes language such as, "I don't have a brain for languages," "My family never could pick up other languages," etc. How does this myth affect how you think about your ability to learn languages?

Magnetic Memory Question #2

What is the "distance" between where you are now with your memory skills and where would you like to be in the future with French? Please be as specific as possible, including something like a deadline for when you would like to see a difference achieved (five minutes from now, tomorrow, next month, next year, etc.).

Magnetic Memory Question #3

What is your education "action plan" for completing the exercises taught in this book so that you have total control over the improvement you would like to see in this area of your life?

Remember: email your answers to me with "French Memory Questions Answered" in the subject line with a copy of your receipt attached to learnandmemorize@zoho.com for a special gift ($24 value).

Chapter 1: How The Magnetic Memory Method Began

Ending The Frustrations Of Rote Learning Vocabulary

Let me tell you the story of how I developed the Magnetic Memory Method and the Memory Palaces for German. Then I will take you through all the steps of that system and show you exactly how it can be applied to French. I will teach you how to set up your Memory Palace system and then give you many examples of how you can populate your Memory Palaces with French vocabulary words.

Let's go back to a wonderful time in my life. I was living in Manhattan. It was an interesting experience, but after nearly two years in the Big Apple, I decided I wanted to move to Berlin. Knowing that I would need at least some rudimentary German to get by in my new city, I attended a number of lessons in a small Manhattan church located in a part of the city that has been historically associated with German immigrants.

The teacher in that school played old cassettes from a learning program called *Warum Nicht?* The teacher showed maximum patience and kindness as her students struggled with the pronunciation, meanings and memorization of the German words, taking turns to repeat what we heard on the old cassettes. I learned very little German sitting in that church.

After moving to Berlin, I did not learn very much German either. It is one of the most beautiful cities in the world and there are German speakers everywhere. I even went to class for six months. Those classes were for four hours a day, five days a week. My serious devotion to learning the language did not help me get the vocabulary to stick. I felt like I had a giant leaky faucet in my head, one that leaked out every new word I was attempting to learn faster than I could learn it.

Not shy of rote learning at the time, I spent hours writing out the same word over and over again. However, this did little more than hurt my wrist. At one point, I even taught myself to write with my non-dominant hand (something I recommend to anyone who wishes to increase their brainpower).

Learning this new writing skill aside, it was frustrating to lose hours and hours of my time on the futile practice of rote learning. In fact, the only word I remember from my time spent rote learning is allmählich. This German word means, ironically, "gradually."

The Search For A Better Vocabulary Memory System

Fed up with memorizing new vocabulary *gradually*, I searched the Internet and libraries for a memory system designed specifically for vocabulary acquisition. I read countless books on memorization skills and listened to a large number of audio programs such as Pimsleur's programs for German and later French.

This was time well spent because I learned a massive amount about the memory and the power of the human mind. Here and there, I have found language tips that were useful to me and will be useful for you also. These resources for memory improvement are included in future chapters. However, I failed to find anything substantial in the mnemonist literature regarding how to memorize the vocabulary of a specific language.

My Requirements For A New Memory System

Because memorizing vocabulary was my main interest, I knew I would have to develop my own method for memorizing the vocabulary of my target language, which was German at the time. I wanted a system that would allow me to:

- Place words in my mind,
- Instantly recognize those words when I heard them spoken or read them in a book, and
- I wanted this system to rely solely on my mind and be available whenever I needed it.

Not once did I dream that such a system would be easy to create or use, but I did believe that once placed into my mind, I would be able to use it without hassle and even enjoy working with it.

As it turns out, building and using the Magnetic Memory Method for vocabulary acquisition has turned out to be much easier than I thought it would be and much more fun as well. I can guarantee that if you give it a try, it will be fun for you too.

Once I had the system of well-formed Memory Palaces that the Magnetic Memory Method allows you to create in place and had been using it for a while, I realized that it could be readily adapted to any other language. Since that time, thousands of people have learned the Magnetic Memory Method in books and video courses and a movement has begun. Although the Magnetic Memory Method is just one part of the current Renaissance in mnemonics and memory skills, I'm proud to be playing a role because I know that the Magnetic Memory Method offers the most complete training on Memory Palace construction that exists, particularly with details on using the Magnetic Memory Method for language learning.

Now let me thank you for granting me the chance to offer the Magnetic Memory Method to you. I want you to learn this unique approach by showing you the exact steps I took throughout my entire journey towards ongoing vocabulary memorization mastery. I want to help you understand the process in intricate detail so that when you are satisfied with your progress with French and would like to try another language (or anything else for that matter), you can easily adapt the system taught in this book to your own purposes.

It's important that you give these techniques a try. Although books in the Magnetic Memory Series have helped many people, many others have looked at what I have in store in them and felt overwhelmed and that's understandable.

However, it is also not necessary. You can accomplish amazing miracles with your memory. Anything someone else has accomplished, you can also.

Learned Skills Versus Memory Stunts

Many of us are familiar with memory stunts. We've either seen someone on television producing long lists of numbers or recalling the names of dozens of strangers they've only just met.

Many readers of this book will probably have already heard the name Harry Lorayne and may have read one of his memory books (they're excellent). Of course, there are many more interesting and excellent authors who write about memory. However, no matter how many authors you read, some people still find it difficult to imagine why they would want to train their brains to remember so much stuff. For other people, the idea of remembering anything and everything they would like is appealing, but they think it involves too much work, or they may worry that they're not creative enough to create the Memory Palaces and images needed to find success with memory techniques.

Let me assure you that what you are going to learn in this book has nothing to do with stunts. It has nothing to do with fantasies of photographic memory, and it has nothing to do with work. It's about effort, to be sure, but effort that is directed, focused and fun. In this book, you will learn how to be more creative so that you can imagine anything and everything you'll need in order to make even the most abstract vocabulary word memorable.

> What you will learn has nothing to do with memory stunts but is fun, creative, and will give you everything you need in order to make even the most abstract vocabulary word memorable.

We are talking about real skills that anyone can learn and develop with a minimum amount of effort. To get really good does takes practice, but the skills themselves are simple to learn and also very fun.

In this book, you will learn the art and craft of the Magnetic Memory Method and how to apply this art to the memorization of French vocabulary. As a result of your positive decision to use your memory in this way, you are going to walk away with a memory that is improved in many more ways than you could have imagined possible.

Breaking The Negative Cycle

As I noted before, many people feel that memorization techniques don't work for them. This is not an attitude I accept.

Why?

I used to share that attitude. Worse, I used to love telling people about my poor memory. You've probably expounded on your poor memory to other people as well.

Please understand one thing: Every time that you put down what Tony Buzan correctly calls your "perfect memory," you are enacting a crime against your own humanity. Because when we tell others that our memory is bad, we essentially train the people around us to treat us as though we do have a bad memory. This reinforces our beliefs about our inefficient memories and becomes a dangerous circle in which your memory gets worse and worse. You can break free from this negative cycle by learning these skills, and when learned and used in the correct manner, these memory techniques will change your life.

Learning A Positive Cycle

"Like a Ten-Speed bike, most of us have gears we do not use."
Charles Schultz

What I tell people who claim they have a bad memory is that memory techniques are like bicycles. Everyone can use them. Not everybody does, but regardless of body shape, and in many cases even with certain disabilities, there are very few of us who cannot get on a bike and ride.

Bikes have adjustable parts, and like bicycles, the memory techniques taught in this book need to be adjusted by the person using them. Just as we need to re-angle the handlebars, or lower the seat on a new bike, the memory systems taught in this book will need tweaking. Once you've understood them and started to use them, you'll find ways to suit them to your brain type and learning style.

There are really four kinds of learning styles, each of which are characterized by the beginning moments of exposure to a new topic or skill.

1) There are learners who want to know **what** something is first, a bit of its history and background.

2) There are learners who want to know **why** the topic is important.

3) There are learners who want to skip the first two items and just get on with **how** a particular thing works or plays out.

4) There are learners who want to know exactly **what to do** as soon as possible.

Because each brain is unique, this book tries to address all of these different types of learning styles at the same time. Some readers may find the introduction a little long, in which case please skip ahead. Some people will get the concept right away and want to take action. There are steps for doing that at the end of the critical chapters that teach the skills in depth. For those who would like to know why all of this matters, although you may not be able to detect the importance on every page of what is sometimes a rather technical manual, you will find that importance in practice.

Ultimately, practice is what matters to all four learning types. For that reason, it's important to know what type of learner you are and approach this book from your unique perspective. No matter what, so long as you learn and use these skills taught in the Magnetic Memory Method and adapt them to your unique way of thinking, you will emerge with a rock solid memorization system that is grounded on the universal principles of memory and yet also unique to you.

Please realize that learning French by memorizing vocabulary is rewarding for reasons that go beyond the importance of this language in the modern world. Using your memory to learn a new language is fun to do. As a form of mental exercise, it sends oxygen-rich blood to your brain improving health and helping to prevent diseases like Alzheimer's and Dementia.

You don't have to drag yourself to the gym to achieve these wonderful brain health benefits. You can work out in your favorite armchair or while driving or sitting at the beach. You can develop your memory wherever you happen to be and practice French with ease because you'll have every word you've learned perfectly organized within the workout gym of your mind. That's the ultimate goal. You want to have the ability to access any word you've memorized at any time so that you can incorporate that power into your other language learning activities.

On that note, we need to talk about something very important. Many people approached the first edition of this book believing that it was a magic bullet that would create fluency for them, and in fact, for many people, the Magnetic Memory Method has proven to be the closest thing to real magic when it comes to making massive strides in language learning.

However, they have a special secret. They have added the Magnetic Memory Method to the "big four" foundations of language learning:

Reading, writing, speaking and listening.

Every day.

That's right.

No memorization in the world will amount to much if you aren't practicing those four fundamentals.

The problem is that so many people can never get to reading, writing, speaking and listening in any meaningful way because …

Yes, you guessed it –

They can't remember any of the words!

When you can't remember words, you can't learn grammar.

So let's think about things this way. It's a kind of formula.

Grammar is an engine.
It runs on the fuel of vocabulary.
Fluency is the highway.

The crazy thing about the engine is that it is built of vocabulary. The more vocabulary you run through its system, the more it builds itself while at the same time propelling itself along the highway of vocabulary.

And reading, writing, speaking and listening?

Those are the gas stations along the highway of fluency where you fuel up with new words.

And the Magnetic Memory Method?

It's the turbocharger you can add to the engine to increase its speed and efficiency by memorizing words quickly, easily and effectively.

The Magnetic In The Magnetic Memory Method

As an important aside, let's look at this term "Magnetic," talk about why it deserves capitalization and what it means for you.

The Magnetic Memory Method uses the term "Magnetic" for two reasons. First, it is about attracting information in a way that makes it stick in your mind for as long as you want. Second, using the other feature of a magnet, the Magnetic Memory Method helps you repel information. In other words, if we go back to the engine and gas metaphor, there will be impurities and you'll want to fire these out of the exhaust pipe as quickly as possible.

Why repel information? For one thing, there are many things that you don't want in your memory. This includes excessive information that causes cognitive overload. The express purpose of using memory techniques is to *ease* cognitive overload so that you can learn more. The Magnetic Memory Method lets you focus on the most important thing - getting only the information you want into your memory so that you can repel the rest.

There's a danger here, however. Some people have made the claim that memory techniques have no place in language learning. They say that people should focus only on the "big four" foundations of reading, writing, speaking and listening. They say that spending time learning and using memory techniques takes too much time and takes language students away from the task at hand. They also claim that memory techniques are "artificial," whereas the foundations are "natural."

However, this binary opposition between the two language learning forms couldn't be further from the truth. For one thing, there's no need to make them mutually exclusive from one another. That would be foolish. Second, mnemonics use your imagination. Where else but from nature does your ability to see and think in sounds and pictures come from? If anything, it's the books, audio recordings and

> **Mnemonics**: A system or device that aids in remembering information.

video programs for language learning that are artificial. Finally, the reality is that all language learning uses some kind of memory technique. You simply cannot reproduce or use words and phrases and grammar rules that you haven't remembered.

Anything that facilitates greater ease, speed and accuracy in your language learning efforts is worth the time and effort so long as you give the time and effort.

Once you've understood and implemented the Magnetic Memory Method as part of your language learning practice, you'll feel its worth in droves.

To this end, ***How To Learn & Memorize French Vocabulary*** will:

- Train you in the basics of using memory techniques in language learning,
- Help you become advanced,
- Give you countless valuable ideas for how to adjust the ancient techniques of memory for your own purposes,
- Show you things I've tried but that didn't work for me (but may work for you), and
- Show you how I have adjusted the techniques in ways that made them more workable that you can model while experimenting on your own.

As you've probably already noted, much of this book is written in a conversational style. As mentioned, some chapters end with a set of action steps that you can use to begin implementing the techniques immediately. There are also chapters that give you plenty of examples of how I work with the Memory Palaces to memorize words so you can model how the Magnetic Memory Method works in detail.

I normally don't wish my students and readers good luck.

Why?

Because, my goal is to give you the tools and skills that make luck irrelevant, I wrote this book so that your storage and retrieval of French vocabulary words is instantaneous, fun, easy and applicable to any other language you choose to tackle. No luck will be necessary if you follow the Magnetic Memory Method laid out for you in this book.

But ... since we're here to learn and memorize French vocabulary, what the heck. Bonne chance!

Chapter 2: Memory Palace History

Before we begin learning to build Memory Palaces, it will serve you well to know a little bit about the history of this practice.

No one really knows whether or not the following story is true, especially given that there are so many variations of it to choose from, but as we'll see, what really matters is that the legend has clues about how to use memory techniques. I suspect it is for this reason that the "origin story" of Memory Palaces has survived.

Back in Ancient Greece, Simonides of Ceos (c. 546-468 BCE) found himself giving a speech at a banquet before a group of distinguished guests. The building collapsed and everyone but Simonides died.

In some versions of the story, Simonides was called out of the banquet by Castor and Pollux, mythical boxers who represent heroism. There doesn't appear to be any reason these two figures called him out of the banquet, but the occasion did save him from being crushed to death.

Regardless of how the story is told, because Simonides knew the secrets of combining images with locations, he knew exactly where everyone in the building had been sitting. In what must have seemed like a miracle to the city authorities, Simonides recounted the name and exact location of every person in attendance. This enabled the families to claim the bodies of their loved ones and give them a proper burial.

It was Simonides' ability to combine the layout of buildings with mentally created imagery that led to the creation of the Memory Palace technique. The major point of the story that we will be referring to many times in this book is that Simonides used location to "store" and "revisit" memorized information.

In fact, much of what you'll learn in this book boils down to the following equation:

Location = Vocabulary
Image = Meaning/sound of the word
Action = Meaning/sound of the word

One of the reasons Simonides was able to recall all of the attendees at the banquet is because he had associated their name with their **location** in the banquet hall. He did this by creating **associative-imagery**, wild and zany mental pictures that he used to almost instantly recall their names. Not easy names like Butch or Tom or Suzy, but Ancient Greek names that usually had many syllables.

Thus, the **crazy images** that Simonides exaggerated in his mind by **amplifying them with colors, sizes and movement**, matched with the mental **locations** of where he stored those images (which was coincidentally where each attendee either sat or stood), allowed Simonides to recall the names of each individual by mentally moving from station to station and "decoding" the images he created.

You can use this same procedure for memorizing the sound and meaning of all the French vocabulary you'll ever need. If you approach the process in just the right way, it's incredibly simple. All you need to do is understand and utilize a simple vocabulary recall equation:

Location = Vocabulary
Image = Meaning/sound of the word
Action = Meaning/sound of the word

This formula is officially called "The Ultimate Memorization Equation" and assuming that you have enough locations in your Memory Palaces and have put a small amount of thought into the mental journeys you can make through them, you can memorize all of the vocabulary that you want.

If you are interested in learning more about the history of memory techniques, I highly recommend reading this webpage:

http://www.mundi.net/cartography/Palace/.

In addition, you may want to check out the fascinating story of Giordano Bruno, who probably was the only Memorizer ever to be burned at the stake:

http://www.magneticmemorymehtod.com/bruno.

Joshua Foer's recent book *Moonwalking with Einstein: The Art and Science of Memory* is also fantastic, but please be advised that this book covers more cultural history than specific guidance when it comes to building Memory Palaces for language acquisition. However, if you're serious about improving your memory in ways that will directly impact your ability to learn French, then you have everything to gain by reading all that you can on the topic and Foer's book is fantastic for that.

About The Term "Memory Palace"

For some, "Memory Palace" is not the sexiest term. Technically, I refer to Memory Palaces as "non-arbitrary space" because ideally, all Memory Palaces are based on familiar locations. If you're gagging at the idea of using the term "Memory Palace," as we'll be doing throughout this book, feel free to find a replacement.

Whatever you do, don't get hung up on the terminology. I once coached on 80-year-old man through email who went on to memorize hundreds of lines of poetry using the Magnetic Memory Method and loads of vocabulary. The crazy thing is that he understood the techniques I teach very well. What was really blocking him was the term "Memory Palace." Only after we got to the root of the problem, and he finally decided to call his Memory Palaces "apartments with compartments," it was smooth – or rather Magnetic – sailing.

The lesson here is that if you don't like the term Memory Palace, come up with a term of your own. Please don't feel that this problem is silly, trivial or unrealistic. We

> If you don't like the term Memory Palace, come up with a term of your own.

humans are a fickle species and sometimes even the smallest change makes a huge difference. As Wayne Dyer often says (quoting Einstein, I believe), when you change the way you think of things, the things you think of change. Although it may not be technically true, the quote demonstrates that our success with so many things in life has everything to do with how we feel about them, and everything we feel stems from how language conditions our experience.

So if using a "Memory Palace" doesn't fire up your engines and motivate you to make massive improvements in your memory, try "Mind Palace," "apartments with compartments" or even use the term in French, which would be Mémoire Palais.

Why We Call Them Memory Palaces

This issue raises the interesting questions of why we call them "Memory Palaces" in the first place. There are many potential answers, but one of my favorites appears in St. Augustine (354-430 ACE). In his *Confessions*, he wrote "And I come to the fields and spacious palaces (praetoria memoriae) of my memory, where are the treasures of innumerable images, brought into it from things of all sorts perceived by the senses."

This passage is important because Augustine points out that in order for Memory Palaces to become useful, we need to combine locations with all of our senses. By putting sensations together with locations, we create "treasure." We make the information Magnetic so that it will come back to us whenever we wish.

You might also find it useful to know that location-based memory techniques appear to have existed before people like Augustine and Simonides worked with them. In her book on the Buddha, Karen Armstrong mentions the use of memory techniques in Yoga that involve associating images with locations. In addition, the contemporary Buddhist instructor Michael Roach has spoken in great detail about how various meditations were remembered by the monks by placing imagery in different parts of the temple.

For example, in a meditation, which asks us to remember that death, is always behind us, monks were advised to place a black dog at a particular part of the temple to remind them of this principle. Every time the practitioner mentally journeys across this section of the Memory Palace, the image of this dog "triggers" the teaching and helps maintain enlightenment.

Later religious traditions like Catholicism would take such ritualistic reminders out of the imagination and externalize them in the form of reliefs or paintings on the walls of their churches in the form of the Stations of the Cross. If you speak with a Catholic person about this, they will usually be able to name each of these with ease. When you have the opportunity to do so, ask them what they see in their minds as they recite them. Chances are they'll be mentally moving from station to station assisted by their real world knowledge of a church structure.

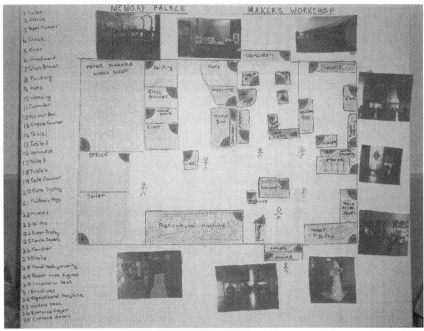

Memory Palace created by a Magnetic Memory Method student in Australia.

PART TWO: THE ART AND MECHANICS OF THE MEMORY PALACE

Chapter 3: How To Build A Memory Palace

In this chapter, we're going to get into a lot of detail about constructing well-formed Memory Palaces, but for now, sit back, relax and let the concept sink in. Memory Palaces will provide you with the ultimate organizational system for learning, memorizing and recalling vocabulary. Think of it as a cheat sheet or crib sheet for your mind.

However, there's one important difference. Using Memory Palaces to store information in your mind is *never* cheating. Some people have asked me over the years about this because they feel that the cutting edge memory "tricks" you're about to learn are unethical, particularly in test situations.

This stems back to the strange notion that memory techniques are "artificial" as opposed to "natural." For example, if you look at other language learning books and listen to podcasts, you'll often find that they use the term "natural language learning." What they mean, basically, is reading, writing, speaking and listening.

Yet, when you think about it, reading and writing and even the language itself is artificial, but the Magnetic Memory Method is based on a combination of buildings that you've encountered in your life and the natural abilities of your imagination to see and think in images by using words. It's the language learning books, video programs and audio presentations that press you to use rote learning and spaced repetition that are artificial. Memory techniques are an organic means of learning information by using more of your mind, not less.

So, *none of this is ever cheating.* Everything you'll memorize using the Magnetic Memory Method has been learned in a legitimate way. You've just learned it faster and more "Magnetically" than anyone else has. Your personal life experiences, the locations you know and your perfect ability to create mental imagery are your "natural" secret weapon. Of course, you can learn a great deal about language learning from those who claim that memory techniques are "artificial," but please be cautious of the argument that memory techniques somehow fall outside of nature. This couldn't be further from the truth.

Magnetic Memory Amplification

That being said, there are three main principles involved in what I call "memory amplification." I use this "artificial" term (wink wink) because memory techniques do seem to "turn up the volume." This louder quality means that the Memory Palaces themselves become kind of like storage unit speakers through which our imagination roars out French words.

In order to learn how to amplify your memory in order to make it more Magnetic, we need to understand three key principles. These are:

Location

Imagery

Activity

Along with these principles, we have the two sub-principles of **preparation** and **predetermination**.

Let's look at them in turn. Keep in mind that each of these principles is individually important and each is interrelated. Use them independently, and they will still help improve your memory. Use them together and your memory skills will soar beyond belief.

Location

Location is part of, but not the entire picture of the Memory Palace concept. At the simplest level of understanding, locations are used to store imagery. We saw how Simonides did this in our story about the birth of the Memory Palace technique in the Western world and the reason we use locations is we tend to remember the structure of places we've lived or visited without exerting any mental effort. At the very least, we use only a minimal amount of energy to recall what our home, school, library or church looks like. The ability to recall the structure of buildings is one of the key principles of memory work: eliminate everything that you don't have to work at remembering and build natural associations.

You might be asking yourself, "What about outdoor locations?" Great question.

For now, I suggest that you work only with indoors locations. Your mind can readily rebuild the layouts of buildings in a way that is much more structured than any forest path or journey down a busy street. You can use outdoor locations after you've worked with at least ten indoor Memory Palaces so that you really know what you're doing and why you're doing it.

As we move through this book, I'm going to suggest that you create a large number of Memory Palaces. Although there are many elements of the Magnetic Memory Method that make it unique in the world of memory techniques, it is the emphasis on multiple Memory Palaces that makes this approach work as well as it does.

Of course, when I tell people just how many Memory Palaces they should build, they think I'm crazy. When you're thinking about locations for storing memories, try doing something that I did for myself when I came up with the Magnetic Memory Method.

I sat down and determined all the places I have lived and all the schools I attended. At that time, I listed eight cities, twenty-five houses (or apartments) and sixteen neighborhoods within those cities. I then added the homes of my friends and family member. There are even hotel rooms that I remember very well in cities that I have visited. The path I took from an apartment in Paris to the Louvre, for instance, has served me very well over the years. I've found that the number of Memory Palaces I can build is exponential. The list expands each and every time I travel or intentionally step into a store I've never visited before.

By intentionally, I mean deliberately deciding that each new building could become a Memory Palace and paying attention to its layout. If you start doing this, you'll have more than enough buildings from your past and present to build all the Memory Palaces you could ever need while adding new ones as part of your future as a Magnetic Memorizer.

Action Step – Start a list of all the locations with which you are familiar.

Why not try this exercise now? Get out some paper and a writing instrument. Start with the first home that you can remember.

Then, list all of your relatives whom you've visited and have houses or apartments you can remember.

Move on to list all of your friends and their homes if you remember them. Do this for both your past and present friends. If you have bad memories from previous relationships, you can leave these out. However, try to be scientific and clinical about it. Just because you may have a bad memory about a particular building, it doesn't mean that you can't "cleanse" it of those feelings and use it for the sake of good.

Next, list all of the schools you attended.
List churches you've belonged to
Clubs
Movie theatres
Shopping malls
Art galleries
Libraries
Bookstores
Etc.

By the time you've completed this exercise, you'll see that we all have more territory in our minds than we could ever possibly hope to use for storing memories. If you haven't already claimed them, there are free worksheets and supplemental guidance just waiting for you here:

http://www.magneticmemorymethod.com/free-magnetic-memory-worksheets/

Grab those worksheets now and get started because I have a lot of other great things on the other side of that link to help you improve your memory. The best part is yet to come once you've taken action and used the worksheets to list your Memory Palaces and complete a few other exercises.

Once you have a list of potential Memory Palaces, you can then organize them in particular ways. You can organize them alphabetically, for example, which is a major suggestion in this book and if you've downloaded the worksheets, you'll have guided instructions

Once we've got our Memory Palaces organized, we can then think deeply about how to best create memorable journeys within them. To do so, we will sub-divide our Memory Palaces into individual macro-stations and micro-stations. Don't worry too much about these terms right now. They are explained more fully in the next chapter.

The point I want to stress is that you *always* use locations with which you are familiar. Many people want to build fantasy Memory Palaces or base them on video games.

I'll be honest with you.

This *can* work.

The problem is that because they're invented, you then have to remember what you invented as you move through the fantasy Memory Palace, and as you move through it, you have to rebuild it in your imagination. When that happens, you'll be spending way more time on your Memory Palace and almost no time on learning French!

When you get this technique right by preparing in advance, you can spend nearly *all* your time on rapidly memorizing as much French vocabulary as you want because well-constructed Memory Palaces based on real locations *ease cognitive load*.

It can't be said enough:

The more you use places you already know, the less you have to remember.

The less you have to remember, the more you can associate.

The more you can associate, the more you can remember.

The more vocabulary you can remember, the more you know.

Try This Exercise Now

Close your eyes and visually reconstruct the room you're sitting in using your imagination.

Chances are that you easily can do so. You might actually "see" it or only see a kind of floor plan made of simple shapes. You may even only "feel" or "sense" the concept of the room, but in one way or another, you can reconstruct the room in your mind.

Don't worry if you can't "see" it as if you were watching HD TV. You can also "see" using descriptive words and thinking about the relationship between points in space.

After that simple task is done, mentally move out into the hallway and reconstruct that space. Move throughout the entire building, recreating its rooms and its nooks and crannies in your mind. Work on making it visual, or simply develop what is now becoming a Memory Palace in whatever way works for you.

We'll talk later about becoming more visual in your imagination, but at the end of the day, we are all visual enough to create a mental construct based on a real location. So if you absolutely cannot see anything in your mind, just think to yourself about moving from place to place (or station to station) using words.

Whether you are mentally seeing or describing in words your emerging Memory Palace journey, you are creating powerful – and Magnetic - "links" between different locations in space. You're going to tag these as "stations" that can be revisited at will with (almost) zero effort.

Once you've established these stations, you can place information at, on, beside, under or in some in these stations. By using a few other tools, you're going to "magnetize" that information (vocabulary) by using associative-imagery. Then, you'll revisit those stations later in order to retrieve the vocabulary you've memorized by decoding the associative-information.

If you're thinking this process sounds involved, complex and requires too much creativity …

Don't worry. You're not alone! Lots of people have told themselves "this will never work for me. My mind is different."

I've warned you already about not falling into the trap of this kind of thinking, and I'll warn you again.

You can build Memory Palaces and you can use them. You just need a few more tools.

You're going to get them. Just keep reading. ☺

Chapter 4: Example Memory Palace

In the previous chapter you constructed a Memory Palace of the room you were sitting in and extended it through the hallway and entire building – the location is established. The next step is to set up the "stations."

As you've learned, we next divide our Memory Palaces into "stations." These stations form the stops along a mental journey based upon "actual" paths that you could take in the real building upon which you've based your Memory Palace.

Everything You Always Wanted To Know About Memory Palace Stations ... But Forgot To Ask

The concept of "stations" is nothing more than an updated take on the Method of Loci. "Loci" means "locations" and the Method of Loci is the art of using them to drop and retrieve information. However, "location" is too broad and is better used to identify Memory Palaces themselves. For this reason, I have drilled down to call these "Loci" stations.

There are in fact two types of stations:

Macro-stations
Micro-stations

A macro-station is an entire room (i.e. bedroom, kitchen, living room, or bathroom). A micro-station is an element inside of a room (i.e. a bookcase, bed, TV set).

It's important to recognize the difference between these two kinds of stations because at the beginning stages of using Memory Palaces, it's often best for people to start out with macro-stations until they get the hang of the techniques. Many people rush too quickly into the game and wind up confusing themselves.

Again, macro-stations are entire rooms. That's what makes them easier to use at the beginning. When you start using micro-stations, we're talking about using beds, chairs, tables and appliances as stations. Without some practice with the bigger rooms first, you risk frustrating yourself.

> A **macro-station** is an entire room (i.e. bedroom, kitchen, living room, or bathroom).

If you don't believe me, then that's a good thing. You'll go out and try using imaginary Memory Palaces or using every windowsill and coaster as stations and fail to get results. Then you'll come back to this book and get yourself back to basics.

> A **micro-station** is an element inside of a room (i.e. a bookcase, bed, TV set).

All that said, many people "get" how the Memory Palace works right away. This intuitive understanding enables them to make quick progress right away with micro-stations. I'll leave it up to you and invite you to email me at any time if you have questions about what you should be doing at learnandmemorize@zoho.com.

Rest assured that I myself still use macro-stations for many purposes. We're not playing a game of "fill up all available space with crazy images so that we can remember every word in the world." We're talking about intelligently deciding what we want to achieve, selecting the right Memory Palaces for the job and then populating them with words in accordance.

No matter what happens as you explore the techniques you're learning in this book, get in touch with your questions. I'm happy to help you. However, you will do both of us a huge favor by first filling out the Magnetic Memory Method Worksheets before emailing. I love helping people, but far too often get emails from people looking for advice that is answered both in this book and by taking action using the Worksheets. They have been designed in such a way that merely by filling them out, you'll have a ton of Memory Palaces at the ready.

If you still need help, I'll be able to help you at a much higher level because you'll have come to me with targeted questions. Without having done some preparatory work on your own, it's kind of like going to a teacher and asking "what is math?" after he or she has given you a set of simple worksheets for practicing simple arithmetic at the end of an hour long class devoted to exactly how the plus and equal symbols work in coordination with numbers.

That hard "coaching" speech dealt with, the most important thing here is to get started ASAP. The sooner you start experimenting, the sooner you can start getting results from these amazing memory techniques. Memory Palaces are humanity's greatest invention. Once you start getting results, you'll see why.

Visual Examples Of Macro And Micro Magnetic Memory Palace Stations

Macro-Station

Have a look at the following diagram.

Each of these rooms represents a macro-station. There are four in total, five if you count the entrance – bathroom, bedroom, living room, kitchen and entrance.

Micro-Stations

The following diagram represents the same home. In this case, I've provided labels that indicate just some of the possible micro-stations in this home:

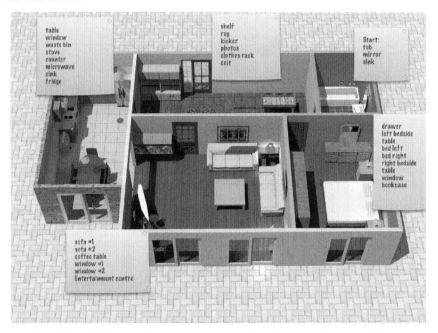

By identifying a liberal amount of micro-stations within each room, we now have 30 individual spots (i.e. micro-stations) upon which to place information that we want to memorize. Again, you want to work up to this level of multiple stations per room so that you can take advantage of Memory Palace journeys that offer this many possibilities. However, do not rush into it without mastering macro-stations first.

Exercise

In order to let the power of building a Memory Palace journey sink in, take a moment to identify the Memory Palace macro and micro-stations in your own home. It doesn't matter if it's a house, an apartment building or a trailer. Even if you're reading this in prison, you can build a Memory Palace using your present location. I know this for a fact because both prisoners and prison guards have written to me to tell me about their experiences using them as Memory Palaces.

To fully benefit from this exercise, I suggest that you:

- Draw your Memory Palace by hand in a notebook
- Create a top-down list

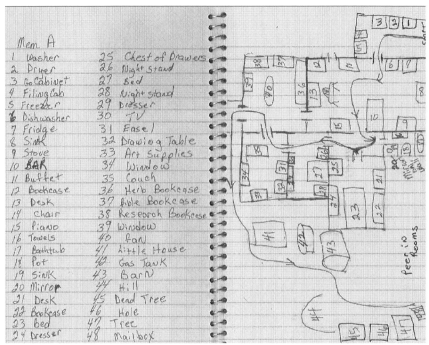

Top-Down List

In other words, tap into both your visual imagination and your conceptual, organizational imagination.

Two Key Principles

As you construct your journey through the Memory Palace by identifying your stations, obey two key principles:

- Do not trap yourself
- Do not cross your own path

You want the journey you create to be linear because this makes it easier to follow the journey in your mind and you will spend much less mental energy when using the Memory Palace to store and recall words.

Moving from the visual example I've given you on the previous pages, let's look now at a real set of micro-stations in a real Memory Palace that I actually use.

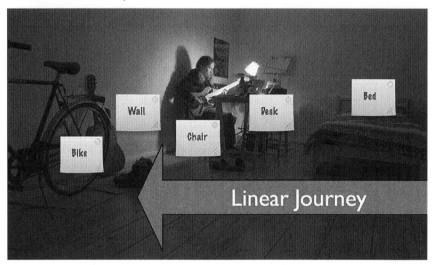

This is the office where I write. The bookcase stores books. I use the bed to study the effects of meditation on memory and research dream recall. I use the desk and chair to write books and work on music memorization, the wall to lean my guitars on and the bike takes me home at the end of the day.

I also use all of these "micro-stations" to store information that I want to memorize. By making the journey linear with no path crossing and moving towards a door so that I'm not trapping myself, there is no confusion about what comes next along the journey and mental energy expenditure is kept to a bare minimum.

Now that you've had a look into just one room of just one of my many Memory Palaces, are you beginning to see the power of separating places that you already know into individual stations so that you can use them to "drop" pieces of information in order to access them later?

I certainly hope so because there is literally no other memory tool this powerful. Now let's learn how to use it.

Okay, I Have A Memory Palace ... Now What?

I'm going to give you several examples of Memory Palaces in action. However, because I want to show you how their use in a complete manner, there are a few other items that we need to go through first.

Here's why:

When using Memory Palaces, we store information on or beside what we have been calling "stations." The question is ... *How? What does this mean?*

What it means is that in order to recall information that is hard to remember, we have to associate it with something that our minds find easy to remember. If I told you that Oedipus is structured with architectonic tautology and features a fabulous example of peripeteia and anagnorisis ... your eyes would probably roll back in your head. You might even scream with frustration if you were asked to recall what these terms mean.

If I told you that earlier today I saw a giant *pear* punch my *pet* dog *Ty* while shouting "ya!" you'd probably be able to repeat that information back to me half an hour later. Especially if I made a big deal out of how huge and green the pear was, how fast its fists moved and how loud it shouted "ya!" and Ty yelled in pain.

Now imagine sticking that image of a giant pear punching a dog named Ty while shouting "ya!" taking place in your bathroom.

Have you done it?

Good.

If not, close your eyes and imagine that nasty pear punching a dog named Ty and shouting "ya!" If you can't see the imagery in your mind, just think about it using words.

Now, take the component pieces and put them together.

Pear + Ty + "ya!" = something very close to peripeteia.

Now just imagine that Ty snaps back and takes a huge bite out of that pear. That would be a reversal of the pear's fortune, wouldn't it?

I'm glad you agree, because "reversal of fortune" is exactly what peripeteia means.

In essence, we've created a vignette that "encodes" the sound and the meaning of the target word we want to memorize. When we come across it again in a Memory Palace, we need only look at the image, break it down into its component pieces to "decode" it and retrieve the memorized word in its original form.

If you can create and imagine a little picture like a pear attacking a dog, leave it in your bathroom so that you can recall the sound and meaning of a word, then you can leave hundreds of words in a structured manner throughout the buildings you are familiar with and make rapid advancements in your French language studies.

There's a bit more to be said about this process, so let's dig in deeper and explain more about exactly what's going on when I suggest that you learn to make images like these so that you can spread them around your Memory Palaces with ease. You're going to learn to combine imagery and action in a particular way that will ensure your success each and every time you study French vocabulary.

Imagery

Imagery is … well, imagery – mental pictures that you build in your mind. For the purposes of memorization, these pictures need to be **big** and **colorful**, and the larger and the more colorful, the better. Essentially, you want to exaggerate the size and colors because that will make the image more memorable. This will in turn strengthen the association.

Some of the students I've taught tell me that they are not particularly visual in their imaginations.

I understand this completely.

In fact, when I used to read a novel, I rarely saw images in my mind. I read the descriptions, of course, but my mind kept the imagery conceptual. It's possible that I had something called Imagination Deficit Disorder or IDD.

Whether I suffered from this condition or not, I don't know. However, I memorized a lot of information using the techniques that you're going to learn without seeing anything in my imagination. In fact, I excelled by using words alone to describe the kinds of crazy images we'll be discussing in this book. We'll talk about some of the exercises I used to become more visual, but for now, rest assured that as a person who previously experienced a low visual threshold, I am able to give my non-visual students in the Magnetic Memory Method Masterclass quite a few suggestions based on my own experiences.

Whatever happens, do not allow a lack of imagination for intense imagery to be a barrier. I know that you can incorporate imagination into your memory work. Here are some approaches and exercises to help you create powerful images in your mind, either at the conceptual or visual-imaginative level.

First, if you can't think in color, don't force it. You can try thinking in black and white. Exaggerate the black and white. How black is the black and how white is the white? Is there an opportunity to use gray in some memorable way?

In the event that black and white patterns are not useful for you, another tactic, one that I have used to great effect, is to associate certain prefixes with actors or fictional characters. For instance, the Spanish prefix cachi- is associated in my mind with Charles "Chachi" Arcola, who was played by Scott Baio on the popular television series, *Happy Days*. The words don't sound exactly the same, but I am able to visualize Chachi and make the association cachi. Thereafter, every word that begins with cachi gets automatically linked with Chachi.

Another option is to use paintings that you are familiar with in your imagery. The more you are aware of their intricacies, the better. The next time you are in an art gallery or looking through an art book, pay closer attention to what you are looking for. The material could become fodder for better associations with the French vocabulary you will be memorizing.

I must mention a small problem with artwork, however. Paintings and statues tend to be static. Unlike actors, you've seen on television and movie screens, painted figures don't move. You'll need to add motion yourself. That being said, if you can imagine the Mona Lisa walking like an Egyptian outside of her frame, or Michelangelo's David doing the Moonwalk, then you should have no problem.

You can also use toys that you remember in the associative-imagery you create. GI Joe, Barbie, My Little Pony … anything goes. As with paintings, the most important factor here is that you can put these figures into action.

With these concepts in mind, here are a number of things you can do starting today to become more visual.

1) Examine how you read. Do you actually "see" what you are reading? This question applies to both fiction and non-fiction.

If you read primarily non-visually, make a determined effort to see the characters and environments in the material you are reading.

Pause to close your eyes and literally build the imagery in your imagination if it isn't coming to you with the desired ease. Don't rush through the pages. Work at this with deliberation. You can start with an imaginary wire frame and pile on the clay if you find a sculpting metaphor helpful, or you can imagine that you are painting the scene. Personal experimentation will demonstrate what works best for you.

2) Examine how you watch films. Are you absorbing all of the visual material, including the backgrounds? By paying closer attention to what can be called the "deep mise en scene" (a fancy term for "background") you will start seeing how filmmakers fill the visual field with hidden imagery meant to shape your viewing experience

3) Visit art galleries. I used to hate art galleries until I realized how useful they are when it comes to developing the visual imagination. Art galleries are also excellent for developing Memory Palaces.

One of the great things about art galleries is that you can see the brush strokes in great detail, something that very few art books allow for. Since so much of memorizing is about experiencing images in process, looking at paintings is an interesting means of seeing movement as a special effect produced by a motionless canvas.

You also get to see the paintings and other artworks in context. You see how they've been framed, how they've been placed in relation to other paintings and how other people are perceiving them as they move around the art gallery. The more consciously aware you become of these elements, the more visually aware you will be.

4) Look at art books. Good art books are great for looking at paintings and other artworks you can't physically visit. You can also spend more time with the images, revisiting them again and again to study their intricacies.

5) Pick an image from a novel. For example, if you're familiar with *Lord of the Flies*, choose the conch. Using an imaginary version of the room in which you currently sit, close your eyes and recreate that object in vivid and intense detail.

It's very important that you create the image in a room of a Memory Palace you've created.

Why? Because using mentally reconstructed locations is the key to all Magnetic Memory Method efforts. You're going to use the Memory Palaces to memorize French vocabulary, so why not practice making images in the same location as part of your practice drills.

In effect, the rooms of your Memory Palace are the canvas upon which you will paint moving objects and figures in your imagination.

Once you have vividly created an image, be it a conch or some other object from a novel (a sword, ring, piece of characteristic clothing or treasure), do the following:

- **Increase and decrease its size**. Make it so huge that it presses up against the walls of the room in your Memory Palace (crack the walls if you like).

- **Next, make that image so small** that it practically disappears.

- **Spend time working on the speed of the transformation** from big to small. Focus on actually seeing the object change sizes.

- **Spin the object in space** - left, right, in every possible direction. Spend time seeing every detail of the object in your mind from every perspective.

- **Mentally push the object around the room**, both forwards and backwards.

- **Shine light on the object**. Reduce the light around the object, again experimenting with the speed at which you imagine the transformations.

- **Change the colors of the object**. Change the outer colors by working with the surface of the object, but also the inner glow. Work with all the colors you can think of, and for bonus points, study a color wheel to become more educated about color combinations.

In this exercise, you've used an object from a novel. This means that you had to invent what the object looked like based on your general understanding of what such a thing should look like. If you chose a fantasy object from a science fiction novel, for example, then your creative work was that much more cut out for you and more rewarding.

You can extend this exercise to using an object from a movie. Doing so allows you to relax your visual creativity because you don't have to "build" it based on an author's description. Borrowing an image from a movie doesn't make the exercise any less challenging and it can be even more rewarding. Follow all of the same steps you used for creating and manipulating an object from a novel with the object you've selected from a movie.

Please put these suggestions into action. They are some of the finest exercises you can engage in if your goal is to easily and quickly learn and memorize French vocabulary.

Action

By now, you will have thought about different locations you are familiar with, the macro-stations within those locations and different ways that you can use exaggerated imagery.

The next step is to give your images a bit of movement (more than a bit, actually). Just as you want to exaggerate the size and color of your images, you also want to exaggerate their actions in order to make your target vocabulary more memorable.

It's not an entirely nice way to think of things, but I have to tell you about a sensitive matter. Something that will work wonders for your memory is to make the action in your associative-imagery violent.

Think about highway accidents. Unfortunately, they serve as the perfect example of how memorable scenes of violence can be – even in their aftermath. If after seeing an accident or accident site you could not shake the memory of your mind, then you know how powerful violent images can be.

This is not to suggest that lives need to be lost in your memory work. Cartoon violence that makes you laugh will work too. Wile E. Coyote, for instance, provides a strong example of someone willing to savage himself in some pretty hilarious ways when trying to make the Road Runner his dinner.

Again, the goal is to create something so potently memorable that working hard to recall the image is unnecessary. It will instantly come to mind when you look for it because you've given yourself no other choice. You've made the image impossible to forget.

Now, you may be thinking that using this technique is going to lead to a brain cluttered with bizarre images. This may indeed happen in the beginning when you are first learning the Magnetic Memory Method. With practice, however, the images you have used will ultimately fall away. You'll still wander your Memory Palaces and have a hankering of what the images were that you used, but they will be secondary. The words and their meanings will be the central artifacts on display. They will be part of your fluency.

Preparation And Predetermination

At this point, you've gotten most of the "big picture" of how memory techniques work. However, there are still two principles we need to cover before moving on to some examples. These are Preparation and Predetermination. Please don't skip them. They are cornerstones of the process.

Preparation involves relaxing the mind. I will share several thoughts about it in the concluding chapter, but for now, please realize that when the mind is tense, busy or exhausted, it will resist attempts at memorization.

Being stressed out does not mean that you won't be able to remember, it only means that your mind won't be in the most receptive state possible to remember. When your mind is open and relaxed, you'll be amazed by how these techniques will double, triple and even quadruple in effectiveness.

Predetermination involves charting out the memory locations and stations in your multiple Memory Palace system *before* making any single attempt to place the words you want to memorize.

I must stress that before populating your Memory Palaces for French, you will want to build the entire system first. Having tried to make up my Memory Palaces as I went along, and helped hundreds of people who have tried the same, I can tell you that this leads to little more than frustration and impoverished results. Please spend the necessary time to predetermine the locations that you want to use and label the individual stations within them. The Magnetic Memory Method Worksheets make this easy for you.

Before continuing, I want to stress that perfection is not the goal here. It's important not to harm your forward movement by being too particular about every little detail. You just want to get the basic layout in place so that you can work relatively quickly with the words you want to memorize. Movement is better than meditation, so please take action and build your Memory Palaces so that you can model the examples you're about to discover on the following pages.

How To Practice Using Memory Palaces With Associative-Imagery So That You Can Memorize Dozens Of French Words At A Time

So far, we have discussed the principles and the terminology of the Magnetic Memory Method and even built a Memory Palace. Before we get into the detailed French vocabulary memorization, let's test out the theory and prove that Memory Palaces are indeed the best and most fantastic way to remember information.

By now, you've also downloaded the Magnetic Memory Method Worksheets and filled them out. If not, do so now before continuing. Here's the link:

http://www.magneticmemorymethod.com/free-magnetic-memory-worksheets/

Now, I want to give you an exercise, but I don't want it to be trivial. Far too many books and articles on using memory techniques tell you that shopping lists make for good practice.

Maybe so.

If you like shopping.

The truth is that you should practice using memory techniques with either:

1) Information that interests you
2) Information that will improve your life
3) Information that both interests you and will improve your life

There's no point in exercising with anything less, the rare exception being memorizing the order of playing cards from a shuffled deck. This highly specialized technique can be incredibly fun for training and can be used to do some stunning magic tricks.

Example – Regions Of France

With that said, I need to give you some kind of example of how to memorize unfamiliar words, so let's practice with just some of the **20 regions of France**. When we're done, I'll give you access to something related that I think you'll find very inspiring.

I will give you three examples for you to model. Please complete the rest of the regions on your own using your first Memory Palace in order to get the full benefit from these techniques. Fun memory drills like this will prepare your mind for memorizing vocabulary. For now you will be memorizing only the sound of the words for these regions. Later you will memorize both the sound *and* the meaning of words.

As you go through this exercise, use whatever associative-imagery that comes to your mind. We've got an entire section on this matter coming up, but for now, read the images I'm going to suggest to you and come up with your own. So long as they are over-the-top, hilarious, zany and memorable, your chances of recalling the names of these provinces will be high. If you relax before and during the process, you'll find that your mind will come up with memorable images that connect with the names of these provinces with ease.

So let's say that you're planning a trip to France. Let's attach some of these provinces to the macro-stations in one of the Memory Palaces you've already created using the Magnetic Memory Method Worksheets. (For the purposes of this example, I'll use the Memory Palace diagram you saw in the previous chapter just in case you haven't downloaded the MMM Worksheets.)

Also, please note that I'll be giving you some examples from my own imagination. These descriptions of images and actions **are for demonstration purposes only**. In order to achieve real results, you'll need to create your own images. Please don't fall for the memory trainings out there that expect you to recreate their images in your mind and succeed.

In all honesty, you might experience some results from my examples, but you can achieve total success in recalling the regions of France if you practice creativity and come up with your own images.

Don't cheat yourself. The examples I'll be giving you in this book won't cheat you either. This book is about teaching you to fish and not about dumping the fish into your boat. When it comes to memory techniques and using them well, you risk starvation if you can't cast your own line to reel in the fish.

With that stern warning out of the way, let's get started.

Just as a reminder, here is the Magnet Memory Palace we are using in this example:

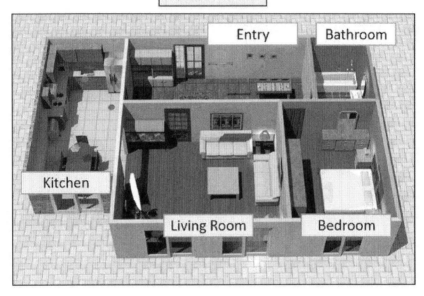

Macro-station 1: Bathroom - Alsace

Imagery: Do you like movie actors? I sure do. Using actors in your imagination is a great way to stimulate your creativity, especially if you deliberately recreate them in your mind the way I suggested you do with popular images before.

Al Pacino is one actor I like in particular.

Action: In my Memory Palace, **Al Pacino** "says" that he **hates the Ace of Spades**. That's why he's tearing one of them to pieces while saying "Al sace."

Al (Pacino) + Ace = Alsace

Macro-station 2: Bedroom - Aquitaine

Imagery: Have you ever seen a theatre play? Chances are you have. So imagine this scenario:

Action: Al Pacino, after tearing up the Alsace of Spades, marches past the bedroom. It's now a theatre stage with a huge curtain. He says, "I quit!" and tosses the torn pieces of the Ace of Spades at the curtain. They make an "Aquitaine" sound as they fly through the air but because the torn pieces are now bleeding, they s"tain" the curtain.

A(**l Pacino**) + (I) quit! + (s)tain = Aquitaine

Macro-station 3: Living room – Auvergne

Imagery: Al Pacino can still serve for this word, but this time he will be carrying a huge letter "O" over his head. That's to help recall that "au" in auvergne sounds like "oh." You can hear the pronunciation of this word (and all pronunciations for the words in this book and many other French words) starting here:

http://www.forvo.com/search/Auvergne/

Action: Al bursts into the living room waving the "O" over his head. He throws it at that funny character Ernest from TV who always says, "You know what I mean, Vern?" Al Pacino makes a loud "ya" sound as he throws the "O."

O + Vern + "ya" = Auvergne

Now, you might be thinking – Wait a minute, these sounds and images are out of order.

And it's true. They are.

However, in our memory efforts, that doesn't matter. We'll be covering how to get the sound and meaning of words into long-term memory in a future chapter. By using a specific fast and fun technique, you will quickly leave these images behind and still be able to say and understand any word at any time and under any conditions entirely from your memory.

~~~

If you can remember simple items like these as quickly and easily as I know you're capable, you can memorize all the French vocabulary you need to converse intelligently.

However, I know what you might be thinking. "This stuff is easy for you, Dr. Metivier. Your imagination is some kind of turbo-charged Energizer Bunny. I'll bet you even used to eat LSD for breakfast."

Except for the LSD part (don't tell my mom), my mind isn't any more or less creative than yours is. The trick is that I've developed it by deliberately engaging in creativity exercises. You can too.

The other trick is taking just a second with each image and making sure that you're really seeing it in large, vibrant and bright colors. Focus on the action. Make it zany and crazy. Make it as exaggerated as possible. Again, if you cannot see in your mind, focus on the words you create. Make the descriptions wild, crazy, and memorable. Merely by doing this, you can become more visual and regardless get great results.

If you're still doubtful that this is going to work, let me introduce you to Daniel Welsch. Although he only gives you a couple of examples to get you started as well, you're going to love this hour-long interview with him from the Magnetic Memory Method Podcast I host. He talks about how skeptical he was about the memory techniques I teach – especially since he's a language teacher himself. Yet, after trying out these techniques for himself, he managed to memorize all 50 Spanish provinces in less than hour.

Use this link to listen to that fascinating interview with Daniel Welsch now:

http://www.magneticmemorymethod.com/how-to-memorize-50-spanish-provinces-on-your-first-go/

Chapter Summary

Choose your first Memory Palace by identifying a familiar location. Many people suggest that you should use your own home as a beginner, but I think you can be more adventurous if you wish. Use your school, church, workplace – nearly any indoors location will do. Keep in mind that you want to make it indoors to maximize the effectiveness, and you want to be familiar with the location to the point that even without revisiting it, you can create a journey throughout the location in your mind and divide the journey into stations.

When working with your first Memory Palace, decide first whether you want to start with macro-stations or get right into using micro-stations. My preference is for people to start large with macro-stations and then narrow in using micro-stations, however, I leave this to you. Ideally, you'll try both, but there's only one first time and it's important not to frustrate yourself if you feel in advance that using micro-stations might be too much.

On the matter of overwhelm, make sure that you construct your first Memory Palace journey in a way that neither traps you nor enables you to cross your own path. This can be admittedly tricky in some buildings and may mean that you need to abandon features that you could otherwise use as stations in order to keep a linear journey that does not lead to crossing your own path or trapping yourself. If you rely upon the principles I've given you in this chapter, your journey will be streamlined, easy to navigate and effective.

If you're worried about not using all available space because you've left a number of micro-stations behind, don't worry about it. In the long run, it is always worth it to lose a few stations in favor of having journeys that are clear, linear and easily navigable. You do not want to lose mental energy, certainly not when you'll be using your Memory Palaces for the purposes of passing exams.

This is why it's important to focus on developing an economy of means, a tight and focused approach to getting what you want when you want it without having to remember anything about the journey you created. This concept of the economy of means works in film and it will work in your mind to create compelling journeys that help you recall all the information that you'll ever need to memorize.

When creating your Memory Palaces, use these important principles to **draw out your Memory Palaces and keep a top-down list**.

This means not only creating the floor plan so that you can see it visually, but also conceptualizing it logistically. By putting the two mental processes together, your mind will "solidify" each and every Memory Palace you create using this process, the beautiful result of taking a few extra seconds to let your brain interact with a location it already knows using more than one perception modality.

As a brief aside, although the hand-drawn floor plan and top-down list I've created above may not be sexy, that's the point. You don't need to be an artist or a graphic designer. You just need to link your mind with your hand in order to create a stronger link between what you will soon rely upon only in your imagination and the reality of that location in the real world.

This brief exercise will also help ensure that you can follow the journey in your mind almost without thinking about it. You want to move from station to station in your Memory Palace in the same way you move from your kitchen to your living room. We base our stations on elements that we are familiar with for the precise reason that we don't have to think about what comes next along the journey. We just mentally go there.

For true success, it's important to think about the appropriateness of the Memory Palaces you choose. As a student, Memory Palaces should always be project specific. This means that you design them in response to specific memory needs. If you need to memorize a number of mathematical formulas, for example, you'll need to put in a few moments thought regarding which locations would best serve math memorization.

Trust me: after years of doing this, I know that it makes sense to put some thought into what purpose your Memory Palaces are going to serve. In addition, because you draw them, you can be scientific and test which kinds of Memory Palaces work better in general, and which work especially well for certain subjects. Here's a key point: what you measure improves. Measure your memory efforts by drawing your Memory Palace floor plans and listing the stations. You'll see your progress multiply, if not explode.

In order to be truly successful when using Memory Palaces to store and retrieve large amounts of information, it's important that each Memory Palace be selected with care. Your Memory Palaces should be project specific. You want the Memory Palaces you use to respond to specific needs.

For example, I've started learning Japanese. To deal with the hiragana, I needed a Memory Palace with 48 stations that were tightly linked together, but not overwhelmingly so. After some thought, I drew a quick sketch of my girlfriend's apartment. Within 5 minutes, I had 48 stations written out in a list and 15 minutes later, I had memorized both the sound and the shape of 15 characters.

It's really that simple, and I have a free 20-minute lesson on how to do it just waiting for you at the link below. Although it's about

Japanese, it will help you better understand the concepts in this book if you're struggling and would like to see them visualized.

http://www.magneticmemorymethod.com/how-to-memorize-japanese-hiragana/

However, as great as that video is, it represents the outcome of many failures. Had I picked a Memory Palace that was too small or even too large and tried to work with it for this particular set of information, my results would not have been achieved nearly as quickly or with such ease.

Thus, we should always work towards having an economy of means in our Memory Palaces. This term comes from the theatre and from film and refers to using the absolute bare minimum needed to express certain features of a story. A character who is depressed is often cramped by the camera to show isolation and despair. A character who is happy or free is given more space. Space is never wasted and has deep metaphorical value in most good movies.

In the world of Memory Palaces, too much space can lead to "decompression." We often want to pack our Memory Palaces tightly in order to maximize, not just the amount of information we can store in them, but also the energy.

How do you learn about this and get it right?

By building and using Memory Palaces.

I can only give you the guidelines.

Only you can undertake the journey and experiment with what works best.

Before moving on, another reason why you want to make your Memory Palaces specific to the information you're trying to memorize is that it helps you track your results. For example, I told you that I memorized 15 hiragana characters in 15 minutes, knowledge that I could easily express because each station is counted. I could then predict how much time I would need for the remaining characters and budget my time accordingly.

Do This Now

1) Create your first Memory Palace using a familiar location.
2) Give it at least ten macro or micro-stations, or a combination of the two. Don't fear the adventure if you want to go whole hog!

3) Make sure that you don't trap yourself or cross your own path as you mentally journey through the Memory Palace and lock those stations down.

4) Draw the Memory Palace.

5) Keep a top-down record.

6) "Rehearse" the Memory Palace journey in your mind in order to ensure that it "works" for the steps to come.

7) If at any time you have questions, feel free to contact me at learnandmemorize@zoho.com.

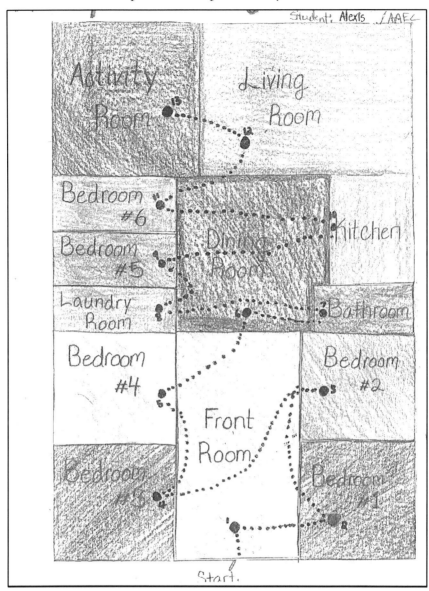

Chapter 5: Example Alphabet Memory Palace

As explained in the previous chapter, it helps a great deal to draw a map of the locations you will be using and have some system for labeling the individual stations. Alternatively, you can list them in a Word document or catalog them in an Excel file. Some students I've had like to actually draw the different rooms or use computer architectural programs to create digital layouts.

Although I personally don't go that far, as suggested, I tend to draw a map of the Memory Palaces. I supplement these with top-down lists in order to maximize the strength of the associations I'll be making within them. Yes, these are extra steps, but I suggest that you engage in them. Let's face it, if you're going to spend time learning a language, you want the vocabulary to stay in your head.

When it comes to creating Memory Palaces, a large part of the Magnetic Memory Method involves associating those Memory Palaces with a letter from the alphabet. This helps us organize the words we want to memorize. If you create an entire system of Memory Palaces based on the alphabet, you can then insert words that go with that letter of the alphabet. For example, all words that start with "A" can go in a Memory Palace based on a building that is itself based on the letter "A."

The less arbitrary the connection, the easier it will be to remember which Memory Palace belongs to which letter and what kinds of words you've stored inside. In fact, it should be brain dead simple to recall that your 'B' Memory Palace belongs to your aunt Bertha, for example, or perhaps you remember a Bingo hall or a restaurant with a name that starts with "B." If you really think about it, you can probably find multiple options for each letter.

That's very good because once you've mastered this technique and tapped out one "C" Memory Palace and you don't want to reuse it, then you can use another building you know that you can attach to the letter "C" in a memorable way.

In order to be perfectly clear, let me show you what I mean when I talk about connecting a Memory Palace to a letter from the alphabet.

Example – Building An "F" Memory Palace In German

The first Memory Palace I ever created for memorizing foreign language vocabulary was my first apartment in Berlin. I had used others while preparing for my doctoral field exams and my dissertation defense, but I made many mistakes. By the time I began learning another language, I was prepared with refined ideas about how to make them work for vocabulary.

My first vocabulary Memory Palace had 8 stations. However, I now recommend and always make sure any new Memory Palace I start working with has at least 10 stations. Once you've gained traction with this method, you can build up to 50 or more. However, to give you the benefit of my perspective, 50 is a good stopping point. You can move outside of a building and add on hundreds of stations, but since writing the first edition of this book, working with hundreds of people and memorizing truckloads of words myself, I find that a 50-station maximum is a sweet stopping point in my mind.

What you do is up to you, but if you're new to memory techniques, keep it simple at the beginning with 10 stations. You can build up later after you've had a taste of the magic.

The first vocabulary Memory Palace I built is on the Feurigstraße. This German word means "fiery street." The name undoubtedly comes from the fact that a fire station is located just a few blocks north of the apartment building.

Making use of the association between the apartment and Feurigstraße, I use that apartment (and every station within its Memory Palace version) to remember words that begin with the letter 'F.' I could use this apartment for any other letter, but this is the association that came to me naturally when I went hunting through my mind for an "F" Memory Palace.

When you work on building your Memory Palaces, it is best to allow for such natural associations to arise and then seize upon them. In my case, because I don't have to spend any time remembering that all 'F' words are connected with the Feurigstraße Memory Palace, I don't have to make any odd leaps in my mind. If I was placing 'S' words in a Memory Palace that begins with or is so closely associated with "F", then it would take my mind a step to search for which Memory Palace has 'S' in it.

As much as possible, you want to eliminate distractions like these by carefully predetermining your Memory Palaces. The more you simplify the system, the more your mind can magnetically leap to the vocabulary you're going to place within them. Again, the less you have to remember about your Memory Palaces, the more you can focus on remembering the images you creat to encode the vocabulary so you can decode it later.

Don't worry. We're going to go into greater detail about all of this later, but for now, **the basic principle is that every location you use as a Memory Palace should start with the same letter of the words that you will store there**.

The Feurigstraße apartment, something I remember well after all these years since I've lived in it, had a nice layout:

My Office
Laundry Room
Bathroom
Bedroom
Wife's office
Living Room
Hallway
Kitchen

Later, I extended this Memory Palace outside of the apartment:
Outside of the door
Stairwell
Front door
Parking garage

Later, when I wanted to extend the Memory Palace, I added:
Sidewalk
Used book store
Playground
Fire station
Church

Sushi restaurant
… and so forth

Don't Forget These Key Principles Of Creating A Powerful Memory Palace Journey

There are two important points that I mentioned earlier but want to stress again at this point. In creating these "journeys" through the stations of your Memory Palace, it's important that you structure things so that you:

Never cross your own path.
Never trap yourself.

If, when you are rehearsing your words or searching for them you have to cross your own path, you are liable to confuse yourself. It is best to create a journey that follows a straight line. With greater practice, this will become less necessary, but in the beginning stages, please keep this important point in mind.

Second, it is important that you don't trap yourself.

The reason I was able to add more stations to my 'F' Memory Palace so easily is because I started at a terminal point in the apartment: my office. Had I started in the kitchen and moved toward my office, I would have trapped myself – unless I wanted to jump off the small balcony and down onto the street.

Doing so would be entirely possible if I wanted to break my ankles, but it is not something I would normally do, and because it is an imaginary action with no connection to reality, this would cause the mind unnecessary work to reconstruct. You want all your energy to go to the unnatural and unrealistic (but memorable) imagery you create for your vocabulary. Don't spend it on flights of fancy with the Memory Palaces themselves. Keep the movement you make through the Memory Palaces as natural as possible so that the exaggerations of size and color and vibrant actions of your associative-imagery truly count.

In the previous chapter, you created a Memory Palace of the place you live in now and made a list of at least 10 macro-stations in either a handmade list or an Excel file.

Decide upon what letter your current Memory Palace will represent. You are going to need 26 Memory Palaces.

Action Steps

For now, here are some actions steps that will help you master the techniques taught in this chapter. Please get started immediately.

1) Locations: Select at least 10 different locations that you remember well. If you are feeling motivated, you can readily list all 26. These could be apartments or houses you've lived in, schools, libraries, workplaces or art galleries. All that matters is that you know them well and can walk around them in your mind. I find that multi-screening room movie theatres work really well for me, and as a film professor, I have over a dozen theatres with which I am intimately familiar. You can also easily download your free Magnetic Memory Worksheets at:

http://www.magneticmemorymethod.com/free-magnetic-memory-worksheets/

Take advantage of this offer right now because these worksheets will help you instantly organize your locations and the stations within them. All you have to do is fill in the blanks. You'll also get free videos and a free subscription to the Magnetic Memory Newsletter, which gives you access to helpful tips about amplifying your memory, inspirational notes, podcasts and links to memorization-related resources that will keep your mind Magnetic for years to come.

2) Macro-stations: Select and list at least 10 macro-stations within each of the locations you listed. Use these stations to create associative-imagery that encodes the sound and meaning of the words you want to learn and memorize.

3) Micro-stations: If you feel you're ready, identify and list the micro-stations within each macro-station. These different micro-stations will become the places you will leave each of the words you want to memorize within each Memory Palace. You could use an armchair and then the lamp table beside it as two different micro-stations, for instance. Even though you will not need to remember any of these individual stations (that's the whole point), you should still write them down for the purpose of testing the strength and rigor of your memorizations.

4) Mentally walk: Take a walk through each Memory Palace. Can you "see" the journey in the different ways we've discussed? Even if you can't "see" them as such, walk through the Memory Palace and make each and every macro and micro-station vivid in your mind.

You can imagine cleaning everything out, if you like, removing all the dust and dirt that can get in the way of your memorization process. What color are the walls? Can you "feel" them? Are they rough or smooth? Is the bed made or messy? Is the armchair stuffed and comfortable or is it wooden and stiff? Are there flowers in the room or maybe a scented candle? Can you smell them?

You get the idea. While making this "walk" it is important to engage as many of your senses as possible.

With that said, I want to repeat for those who feel that they're not visual that you do not need to see the images in your mind in order to get great results. If you'd like an interesting take on exactly why you are more visual than you might think, check out my interview with Dr. Jim Samuels.

http://www.magneticmemorymethod.com/dr-jim-samuels-talks-about-how-to-reduce-stress-with-mnemonics/

In this exclusive interview, Dr. Samuels will convince you that you are the most visual person you'll ever meet.

5) Draw maps: Creating visual representations of each location and the stations within them can be very powerful and save you a lot of testing time later. You definitely don't want to be vague about what comes next in the journey through your Memory Palaces so please make them concrete the first time around using every available resource. Again, using an Excel file is a great idea if you are not a visual person, though drawing the Memory Palace and creating a top-down list is highly recommended.

Here is an example of a hand-drawn map and a top-down list created in Excel:

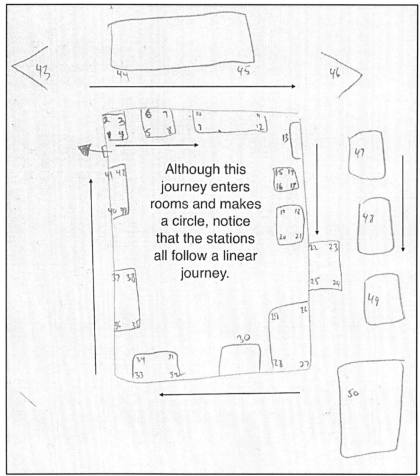

Although this journey enters rooms and makes a circle, notice that the stations all follow a linear journey.

Hand-Drawn Map

Brock High School Memory Palace for B Spanish Words	Station	Word	Main Meaning	Mnemonic
1	Mr. Hermanson's French class	bajo	short, low	sheep driving a j-shaped back hoe (baaaaa)
2	"	barato	cheap	sheep selling rat a cheap toe
3	"	bastante	quite	sheep telling his aunt(e) "that's quite enough!"
4	"	bastar	enough	same with star crashing down on their heads
5	Mr. Andrew's English class	beber	to drink	sheep drinking air jordans with Michael Bay
6	"	bebida (f.)	drink	
7	"	bicicleta (f.)	bicycle	
8	"	boca (f.)	mouth	Beau cawing as a crow crawls from his mouth
9	Gym	bonito	nice	Beau is in a nice suit saying "Beau's Natt-o"
10	"	botella (f.)	bottle	Robot kissing Ella Fitzgerald
11	"	brazo (m.)	arm	Magician Gazzo dangling a bra from his arm

Top-Down List

Have Fun!

Look, let me be straight with you. If what you've been reading sounds like pulling teeth and you already know that you're convinced that you're not going to enjoy it after at least giving it a try, return this book for a refund. Spend the money on index cards and spaced-repetition software instead. *I've heard from a dozen or so people* who genuinely prefer that to using memory techniques and I applaud them if that's what gets them results.

With that said, *I've heard from thousands of people who hate wasting time on index cards and spaced-repetition software.*

I can't blame them. I call those tools the "blunt force hammers" of language learning. Again, if they get you results, by all mean use them, but for those of us who get zero results, the Magnetic Memory Method is worth your serious attention. I'm convinced that if you give it a try using *all* of the tools in this book (by which I mean you should read it all the way to the end and then start over and follow the step-by-step method outlined), you'll find that the Magnetic Memory Method is not only fun, but it's downright addictive!

Test Your Memory

Speaking of fun, give yourself an exam. Nothing feels better than seeing the results of vocabulary memorization emerge from the "thin air" of your newly magnetized imagination.

As I have stressed, you really need to write everything down for the purposes of testing. This means writing down the station, the words and the images you used to encode those words, both their sound and their meanings.

Rest assured, this is not rote learning. It's a one-time method of giving you the ability to double-check what you've memorized.

To make sure you do this form of testing correctly, don't look at the original list you created. Write out everything fresh and then compare the list you wrote out from memory with the original. Think of it as if you're taking a closed-book test. You have isolated yourself from the source information and it is only afterwards can you see how well you fared.

This procedure is important because it forces you to draw the memorized words directly from your imagination, with no peeking at the list you created. You have to pull each word directly from your mind.

There will be mistakes.

Don't sweat it. You'll be using compounding to tidy up those mistakes and weaknesses in your associative-imagery later.

However, you won't be able to make repairs at all if you haven't sufficiently tested the associative-imagery in your Memory Palaces.

Teach

The best way to learn a technique is to teach it to someone else. Why? Teaching is an opportunity to process your knowledge in a completely different way. Consumption and practice is one thing, explanation is a completely different matter. By discussing your newfound Magnetic Memory know-how as often as possible, this will deepen your familiarity with the techniques and prove to yourself and others that these techniques really do work.

Best of all, it's not showing off to do so. You're simply showing people how something works the same way you would explain to your friend the features of a new car or refrigerator, except you'll also be giving them the gift of that car or appliance. You'll be making the world a better place because you'll be enabling others to use their minds more effectively.

Make working on your own memory and helping others improve theirs a habit for life. The more memory you give, the more memory you will receive.

PART THREE: FRENCH VOCABULARY MEMORY PALACE CREATION

Chapter 6: Applying The Main Principles To Learning And Memorizing French Vocabulary

This chapter explains the complete system for creating and using your 26-letter Memory Palace system. By this time, you have already created 10 Memory Palaces, if not more, and charted them out either on paper by drawing maps and/or using the Magnetic Memory Method Worksheets.

If you haven't already collected them, please go here now:

http://www.magneticmemorymethod.com/free-magnetic-memory-worksheets/

Assuming you have them, you have also already identified at least 10 stations within the Memory Palaces you've created.

Here's how I work whenever setting myself up to memorize the essential vocabulary I will need to operate in a new language.

Create The Files

First, I create a folder for each letter.

Name		Date modified	Type	Size
A		3/25/2015 7:08 AM	File folder	
B		3/25/2015 7:08 AM	File folder	
C		3/25/2015 7:08 AM	File folder	
D		3/25/2015 7:08 AM	File folder	
E		3/25/2015 7:08 AM	File folder	
F		3/25/2015 7:08 AM	File folder	
G		3/25/2015 7:08 AM	File folder	
H		3/25/2015 7:08 AM	File folder	
I		3/25/2015 7:09 AM	File folder	
J		3/25/2015 7:09 AM	File folder	
K		3/25/2015 7:09 AM	File folder	
L		3/25/2015 7:09 AM	File folder	
M		3/25/2015 7:09 AM	File folder	
N		3/25/2015 7:09 AM	File folder	
O		3/25/2015 7:09 AM	File folder	
P		3/25/2015 7:09 AM	File folder	
Q		3/25/2015 7:10 AM	File folder	
R		3/25/2015 7:10 AM	File folder	
S		3/25/2015 7:10 AM	File folder	
T		3/25/2015 7:10 AM	File folder	
U		3/25/2015 7:10 AM	File folder	
V		3/25/2015 7:10 AM	File folder	
W		3/25/2015 7:10 AM	File folder	
X		3/25/2015 7:10 AM	File folder	
Y		3/25/2015 7:10 AM	File folder	
Z		3/25/2015 7:10 AM	File folder	

Then I create multiple Excel files. Excel works the best because it eliminates the need to build a table. However, you can just as easily build a table using Microsoft Word, Pages or other word-processing software you happen to be using.

	A	B	C	D	E	F
1				Memory Palace for A French Words		
2	Alan's House	Macro Station	Micro Stations	Word	Main Meaning	Mnemonic
3		1 Alan's Bedroom	1 Dresser	abbatiale	monastery, particularly one headed by an abbot. It can also refer to a church that just happens to belong to a monastery.	Abraham Lincoln and George Bataille having a fistfight in front of a monastery wearing mini-skirts
4						
5			2 Bed			
6			3 Nigtstand			
7			4 TV			
8			5 Bookcase			
9		2 Upstairs Bathroom				
10		3 Staircase				
11		4 Living Room				
12		5 Dining Room				
13		6 Kitchen				
14		7 Front entrance closet				
15		8 Front engrance guset bathroom				
16		9 Front entrance				
17		10 Driveway				

In this case, the files you need to create correspond to the letters of the French alphabet. Below is an example of the alphabet with my locations:

A = **A**lan's House

B = **B**rock Video Store

C = **C**atherine's House

D = **D**awn's House

E = **E**scapades Roller Rink

F = **F**iona's House

G = **G**ary's House

H = **H**enry's Apartment

I = **I**kea

J = **J**ustin's House

K = **K**atrin's House

L = **L**yle's House

M = **M**ike's Apartment

N = **N**ora's House

O = **O**ld Spaghetti Factory

P = **P**reston's House

Q = **K**wiki Mart

R = **R**ick's House

S = **S**amantha's House

T = **T**revor's House

U = **U**niversity Library

V = **V**alleyview Beer & Wine

W = **W**histler Ski Lodge

X = **X**avier's House (Yes, I actually know someone with this name! But his last name is Faucher, so sometimes I use his house for the letter F)

Y = **Y**anina's House

Z = **Z**oo Front Entrance & Parking Lot

It is very important that you have at least 10 stations assigned to each of the Memory Palaces you have selected based on locations with which you are very familiar. Remember, design your passage from station to station in such a way that you do not cross your own path and so that you do not trap yourself. You always want to leave yourself with the ability to add another 10 stations in each location.

Keep in mind that 10 stations is a number for right now. Later you can expand to as many stations as you like per Memory Palace.

As you are trying to come up with each location to link with each letter, let yourself relax. Your mind has the perfect associations for you so long as you don't force it. If you can't think of something that is totally fitting, such as Whistler Ski Lodge for W, just let your mind do its work and go with whatever feels right.

You do not want odd or awkward associations that cause you to stumble in your thinking. You want the associations to be natural so that you can move fluidly through your mind when searching for the words you have remembered.

When it comes to speaking and understanding what you hear, you will sometimes need to do this in real time, so it is very important not to hinder yourself by using forced associations that you will forget and struggle to work back into your memory. That will take the fun out of everything.

What About Memorizing Grammar?

This book does not purport to teach the memorization of grammar.

As the title of this book suggests, you'll be learning to memorize French vocabulary, i.e., verbs, nouns, adjectives and everything else that counts as a word. You also get some notes on memorizing grammar.

However, grammar is its own topic and memorizing its principles using the Magnetic Memory Method does not vastly differ from the suggestions given in this book. If you're looking for a great French grammar learning resource, the best I know for a quick, but in-depth study of French grammar for beginners is *French Grammar for Beginners Level A1* by Kerstin Hammes.

Kerstin, as my friend, is a great teacher and offering readers a special discount on her course. Use coupon code ANTHONYSENTME at https://www.udemy.com/french-grammar-for-beginners-level-a1/ if you're interested in taking her French grammar course. It comes with a 30-day guarantee so if you're not satisfied for any reason (which I doubt will happen), simply request a refund within 30 days of purchase.

However, I do have a few tips for the conjugation of verbs. This involves creating a special Memory Palace just for grammar rules. I offer these ideas to you and hope you can find a way to apply them to memorizing French.

When it comes to French verbs, French speakers add a different ending to the verb depending on the gender and or number of people speaking.

Here is how I have gone about memorizing the different endings, beginning with the place that I use for conjugating verbs: a school where I once taught. I use:

The kitchen

My office
The third classroom
The computer lab
The main hall
The second classroom
The reception desk
The first classroom
The front door
The outside hall
The staircase (it's a small school).

This school was particularly appropriate for me to use because my colleague who owns it is from Argentina and is a native Spanish-speaker. If you are a student, perhaps you will want to use the school where you are learning French as part of strengthening your grammar associations.

The first thing to notice is that I have started in the kitchen because it is in the very back of the school. This way, I can move in a more-or-less straight line through the school without ever crossing my path or becoming trapped. Should I want to add more information to this particular palace, I have created it in such a way that I simply need to step out the door, walk past the veterinarians, the sun-tanning salon, the barbers, the dry cleaners, etc.

Before I describe how I use this particular palace to help remember grammar rules, let's take a brief look at verb conjugation in French.

Verb Conjugation - Écrire

"Écrire" means "to write" in French.

If you want to say, "I write," you need to conjugate the word to "écris" (j'écris).

If you want to say, "You write," you need to conjugate the word in the same way.

However, when "he speaks" and "she speaks," the word becomes "écrit."

"We write" needs "écrivons."

"They write" becomes "écrivant."

To remember that "I" and "you" frequently end with "s," I see myself in the kitchen jumping up and down on a sandwich.

To remember that "he" and "she" often end with a "t" sound, I see a Canadian Mountie exclaiming, "Tea time!" as he waves goodbye in classroom number 3. He has a huge teacup in his hand, and this itself has "T" on it.

To remember that "we" usually ends with "ons," I see myself with a group of students in the computer lab. "We" are marveling at the operating system on a new computer the school has purchased. It has a huge "on" button, and its surface is bursting with light to the point that it is burning our eyes.

To remember "they" often ends with "ent," I have a sign on classroom number two that says "ENTer" on it. A cat I used to have as a pet is also seated on the floor beneath the door, meowing away. I used to call her E.N.T., which was short for Extreme Noise Terror. True story. This is exactly the kind of memorable element that our minds can bring to us as memory aids when we step out of the way and let the associations rise.

Finally, for an excellent online French conjugation resource, visit:

http://www.conjugation-fr.com/

We have dealt with only the basics of grammar and some memorization techniques. However, this site will break down any verb into its Indicative, Subjunctive, Conditional, Imperative, Infinitive and Participle components and then tell you the verb's Simple Past, Imperfect, Future, Past Perfect, Pluperfect and Past Future incarnations in each (where relevant). The website is a powerful tool, so please don't overlook it.

Gendered Nouns

Whenever we learn a new noun in a language that uses gender assignments and place them in our Memory Palaces, it is important that we immediately memorize its gender. This is easily done.

French uses feminine and masculine indicators. "Le" is for masculine nouns and "la" for feminine nouns using the definite article. For the indefinite article, "un" is masculine, "une" is feminine and "des" is used to indicate either words that can take both genders or something in plural.

In my Memory Palaces, I associate:

all ***masculine*** nouns with a boxer – boxing gloves

all ***feminine*** nouns with a skirt

As a quick note for those studying different languages, you might sometimes encounter neutral nouns. In the case of German, for example, I have used fire to remember the neutral nouns.

For example, to remember that "fruits" (fruit) is masculine and therefore "le fruits," I see a pineapple wearing boxing gloves.

To give you an example, consider the feminine noun "la lune" (the moon). It's a simple matter to see the moon wearing a skirt. To make this already zany image, even more ridiculous, I can imagine that the man in the moon is wearing the skirt.

In German, T-Shirt is neutral, so I would imagine a T-Shirt on fire to remember that it would be called "das T-Shirt."

The beautiful thing about taking care to associate every noun with its masculine, feminine, or in the case of German a neutral signature is that you've already given yourself the basis for a crazy image. What could be crazier than a T-Shirt on fire?

You can apply these principles to French starting immediately.

Another Method for Storing Gender

To be as complete as possible, here's an idea I have heard several people discussing. This procedure has never worked for me, because I find it too messy. However, that does not mean you won't find a way to use it.

Instead of having gender nouns stored in Memory Palaces based around the alphabet, some people pick a city and use it as one large Memory Palace. They then divide the city into two parts: masculine and feminine (or in the case of a language like German, into three parts to include neutral noun assignments).

The problem with this method is that cities are expansive. You have to recreate too much information each time you're looking for a word. The paths are indistinct and it's hard to impose structure.

Remember: The less you have to remember about your Memory Palaces, the more vocabulary you can memorize.

Conclusion

To conclude this chapter, here is a list of action steps for immediate implementation on your journey toward memorizing French vocabulary:

Don't do anything until you have fully and clearly understood how to use location, imagination and action in order to effectively memorize at least ten items.

Take your time creating the individual locations and stations within the locations. Your mind has everything that you need so long as you can push your critical mind aside and let your creative mind work. Please realize that it is not absolutely necessary to devise all 26 Memory Palaces straight away. I prefer that my memory students have their Memory Palaces set up in advance so that they are ready to pop new words in without thinking about the process when they want to memorize a word. However, I know that some people want to focus more selectively on just the letters A through H. Such deliberate focus is perfectly fine too.

Ensure that your journey in each and every Memory Palace can be undertaken without crossing your own path or getting trapped. It is tempting to think that one can get away with circling around the forward trajectory of a path, but in the long run, this will only confuse matters. Strive for clear, crisp and direct journeys so that you don't need to think about what belongs where. Remember, the fewer things you have to remember, the easier it will be to recall the words you've placed in your Memory Palaces.

Use Word, Excel, or a handwritten document for each Memory Palace. Start with the first location and proceed linearly from there. Don't forget that the purpose of this part of the process is twofold. First, preparing a written record will help you build your Memory Palaces with much greater detail than doing it in your imagination alone. Second, your written record will allow you to test the words you have placed in your mind.

Examine the grammatical variations of the words you've chosen to place in your Memory Palace. Will you need to remember the gender? Is it a verb that will need declension? Allow your imagination to take the principles you have been learning from this book and show you the best imagery for memorizing these different structural elements of any given word. Use relaxation to facilitate the process.

At the risk of being repetitive, please make sure that you are using the location, imagination and action principles. I mentor many people and a significant number of them report or demonstrate that they've fallen back on rote learning. They are repeating the words to themselves again and again rather than using the Magnetic Memory Method they've learned from one my books, the Magnetic Memory Method Masterclass or personal coaching.

Believe it or not, but both the mind and the body find learning by rote very stressful. The stress contributes to fight or flight responses with leads to frustration and ultimately failure. Unfortunately, many people literally flee from the learning experience.

That's why in the upcoming chapters describe a number of supplementary exercises that you can use to train your memory in greater depth if you feel that you need more training in a relaxed manner. I can tell you that if I hadn't gone through those exercises myself, I never would have devised the 26-letter Memory Palace system in the first place, let alone developed any skill with acquiring a second and third language. They may not seem related, but think of it as the relationship between push-ups and boxing. Pushing the floor away from the body is one of the best ways to strengthen your punch, even though it's a completely different movement.

Learn the genders of every word right away. Decide upon what will signify masculine and feminine and use them consistently. This will become second nature. You don't have to use a boxer and a skirt. Go with whatever your imagination brings to you naturally.

Decide upon a focus. I recommend that you make adjectives a priority, but only after mastering the words that interest you most from a word frequency list. You can use this one to find words that will come in handy:

http://en.wiktionary.org/wiki/Wiktionary:Frequency_lists/French1000

Nouns and verbs are great and you will need them, but adjectives allow you to flavor your speaking and deepen your understanding of innuendo and metaphor. When you do work with verbs, pick strong verbs and learn more than one version of each (instead of just "run," also learn "jog" and "sprint"). As for nouns, use a Visual Dictionary to find your words. This will help you be more selective in the words you choose and give your imagination more fodder for making memorable associations.

For bonus points, try this amazing technique for creating a pool of words to learn in French:

- Record yourself having conversations throughout the course of the day.

- Listen to the recording and make note of all the words you don't already know in French.
- Find out what those words are in French.
- Memorize them using the Magnetic Memory Method.
- Practice proper recall.
- Use those words in speaking and writing the language and look out for them in the material you read and to which you listen.

I get criticism from my friends in the language-learning field about this approach. However, they all admit that they haven't actually tried it! There is often gold to be found in the mines that other people dismiss without first digging a little into the soil.

So if language-learning experts won't even try it ... why should you?

You should try this because you want to be able to express yourself in your target language, and what better way to do that than to study how you express yourself in your mother tongue?

Of course, there often won't be a one-to-one correspondence between what you say in your mother tongue and how it plays out in French. Nonetheless, please don't miss out on this amazing language learning technique. It can really change the playing field for you.

Here's another controversial technique:

Sit with a dictionary as often as possible. When you have worked out your 26-letter Memory Palaces in advance, you are literally going to siphon the dictionary into your mind. Although many words may fail to capture your interest, there is no need to fight with them. Simply find the words that interest you the most or that you think will be the most useful and focus on them. Even if you skip a dozen words in a row, you can always go back to them. Focus on steady progress rather than being a completionist. Never allow frustration to enter the picture.

Many words you will encounter can mean several things at once. Focus on just one meaning at a time. You can always go back to gather more meanings (see the chapter on compounding).

Go to the library, Netflix, YouTube or a store that sells DVDs and stock up on French-language programs. You are going to be amazed and proud of yourself by all the words you'll already be able to recognize and inspired to keep going and memorize more. You can still watch the films with the English subtitles on, or even better, watch them with French subtitles or French closed-captioning on. Mixing Memory Palaces with as much immersion as possible will make for great strides in your learning. Likewise, you can listen to French audiobooks, read French comics, seek out bilingual editions of famous French-language novels (like *Don Quixote*) and listen to French-language music. There are endless possibilities and you'll be glad that you have taken this extra step.

Be careful that the images you use actually help you remember the meanings of the words. It's a painful experience to have installed familiarity with the sound and spelling of a word, only to forget what it means. It is one thing to remember how a word sounds thanks to some crazy imagery, but if you can't remember what the word means, then your time, effort and energy have been lost. Please see the following chapter on compounding for additional ideas on how to make sure you never forget the meaning of the words you have learned.

The most important thing is you take what you've memorized into the realm of speaking, reading, and writing.

Fluency is achieved by knowing words
and
using those words in as many different ways as possible.

Chapter 7: Notes On The Creation And Management Of Your French Language Memory Palaces

Preparation

French vocabulary is rapidly acquired by learners who are prepared with the necessary number of Memory Palaces. We've already talked about some of the points covered in this chapter, but I want to devote a special section to creating and maintaining the Memory Palaces in order to add depth and detail to the process.

Every location you have identified should have at least 10 stations ready to be populated with the association-rich images that will bring the words you have learned easily to mind. You should have created the Memory Palace in such a way that you will never cross your own path or reach a dead end. You always want to be able to add more stations. It is unlikely that you will ever need more than 100 stations in any given Memory Palace, but if ever you do, be prepared to have places to add them.

Some people tell me that it is impossible for any given Memory Palace to have so many stations. However, if you think of all the places you've lived it will quickly become clear to you that the possibilities are endless. If you can squeeze just 10 stations out of your current home by using individual rooms and doorways, with a little thought, you can extend that to 20. How do you walk to the bus stop? Surely, there are numerous memorable locations on the way: the bakery, the florist, the dental clinic above the hearing loss center. If you take the subway, each stop can become its own station where you leave an image. For years, I have used the Toronto, New York and Berlin subway systems as Memory Palaces and each provide countless stations where I leave words that I want to remember for easy recall.

Remember: preparing and predetermining your locations and stations in advance is of the utmost importance when it comes to rapidly acquiring a large vocabulary. Please spend the time creating your constellation of Memory Palaces before placing even a single word of French vocabulary in your mind.

The next matter of importance is relaxation. Please see the final chapter for information about that.

Maintenance

Next is the matter of maintenance. At the risk of being repetitive, I have included this information twice in this book. In Chapter 12, you will find an extended discussion regarding the maintenance, testing and recall of the vocabulary you learn. The French alphabet has 26 letters. Our months have either 29, 30 or 31 days in them. This means that you will always have plenty of time for rehearsal.

I schedule monthly maintenance sessions loosely based on the number of Memory Palaces. Take November, which has 30 days. Day 1 is dedicated to the letter A, Day 2 to the letter B and so forth. If there is a letter with a large number of words I have memorized (some of my letter Memory Palaces have 100-200 words), I assign more than one day to wandering through those particular Memory Palaces. Doing this is well worth the effort and it strengthens your familiarity with the language because you can begin to see patterns and the interconnectedness of the French language.

Although your memorization of the vocabulary has lasting power, it is important to perform "quality control." This means revisiting the words you have memorized at least once a month. It's easy enough to do. You know where you keep all your words beginning with the letter A. It's just a matter of wandering through the A Memory Palace.

How To Use Memory Palaces In Conjunction With Spaced Repetition Software

Although spaced repetition software (SRS) equates to rote memorization, there is a way to incorporate its use if you like the idea of spaced repetition software. If you are not getting the results you desire with SRS alone, then consider hybridizing your flash cards with a Memory Palace.

Here's how:

B MP St. 3

le babeurre

As you can see, the top-right of this card says "B MP St. 3." This indicates this Memory Palace is for words that start with B and that imagery for "le babeurre" is waiting to be decoded at the third station. You can do this on real index cards or SRS cards.

If you like spaced-repetition software, you get the best of both worlds with this hybrid technique: mnemonic assistance and automated repetition based on familiarity. Because SRS filters out words you've declared as familiar, you also don't have to come across them again and again as you do in a Memory Palace (not that that is a bad thing). Of course, Memory Palace work keeps you honest. After all, who hasn't declared that a word or phrase has been learned and let the software sort it away when in your heart of hearts you know you have not learned the word well?

The major con of using SRS with a Memory Palace is you won't be using the *full* powers of your imagination or exercising it to make it stronger. The Memory Palace journey utilizes and strengthens your imagination and ability to recall words instantaneously. Although it might seem like a pain to go over words you already know as you rehearse a Memory Palace journey, the advantages are immeasurable with regard to the ability to recall words. Missing those words on your SRS device is kind of like skipping the first ten pushups because they are easy. The truth is that you cannot lose by quickly revisiting words you've already memorized because you're exercising your memory, not just your fluency.

At the end of the day, this hybrid approach is just a method like any other. Try it out. If you enjoy it and experience results, rinse and repeat. If not, either experiment with adapting it or move on. Stretching a little by learning a new technique is good in and of itself and provides many additional creative benefits for your imagination.

Chapter 8: Example Memory Palace For the Letter A

I was once blessed with living down along a forest road. I'm not sure why my mind selected this house for the letter A, but I always think it best to go with whatever comes naturally. As I spent over a decade living there, my mind is very familiar with the location and it is therefore easy to go through and chart out a number of locations for placing French vocabulary words.

Here are some of the stations, the words I have placed there and a description of the images I used to learn and memorize the words. But first, I should explain that when doing memory work within a palace, I often like to group words together, at least when beginning with a new language.

In the examples that follow, I am focusing only on words that begin with "ab." This helps me use a famous figure to structure my journey through the various locations. The figure I use for "ab" words is Abraham Lincoln. I chose him because, when you think about it, he is already strange and memorable. At the very least, the images I can create by using him will definitely be strange because in nearly all cases, he will be completely out of context.

The followings examples sometimes include some rather weak entries. I'm letting you see them so that you can better understand how the principles taught in this book work and also get a strong feel for what doesn't work and, more importantly, why they don't work and what I've done to correct the problem.

1. Main Bedroom: Abbatiale

An "abbatiale" is a monastery, particularly one headed by an abbot. It can also refer to a church that just happens to belong to a monastery.

To memorize abbatiale, I need to use Abraham Lincoln in some interesting way. This will prompt the fact that the word begins with "ab."

As it happens, one of my favorite French writers is named Georges Bataille. Thus, it is easy to see Abraham Lincoln and Bataille having a fistfight in front of a monastery. Because abbatiale is a feminine noun, the image is made all the more ridiculous by envisioning both of them wearing skirts. I think I will make them mini-skirts just to amp up the hilarity of the image.

Before continuing, I want you to notice something about this example, a point that will reveal how the mind works and how you can capitalize on it.

It is probably a mere coincidence that I chose Bataille for abbatiale due to the similar spellings. It is also coincidence that I happen to use a skirt for all feminine nouns. However, Bataille often wrote erotic fiction, and seeing him in a skirt reminded me of this. My mind has already compounded the image for me.

The lesson here is that whenever performing your memorizations, always keep your eyes – or your mind – open for little coincidences like this. They will make the words you are trying to remember even more memorable, and also add a natural element to the mix.

2. Bathroom: Abeille

Abeille is an interesting word. It means "male bee," particularly a drone bee that carries out particular tasks for its colony, and yet it is a feminine noun. It's pretty easy to remember a giant male bee wearing a skirt, and to get the "beille," I can try having this bee punching a huge bell. Have you ever seen such a thing take place in a bathroom? Probably not.

Let's say that you want to add the fact that this is killer bee. You would then call this bee "abeille meurtriére." "Meurtriére" is very close to the English word for murder, and to get the "iére" sound, I have the bee attacking the bell with a metal tray.

Notice that in this example, my mind has skipped including Abraham Lincoln. That can be a good or a bad thing. In general, I tend to overlook such omissions whenever the artificial construct isn't needed. As always, we use the training wheels when we need them. When we don't, they can become counterproductive. If you practice memorization by using relaxation, you will find that the artificial devices either apply themselves naturally, or you won't need them at all. Please bear in mind that I don't mean to confuse you with contradictions in the method. I am only pointing out that flexibility is key.

3. Laundry Room: Abiogenèse

This is a cool word. Abiogenèse refers to the spontaneous evolution of life from inorganic material. Biogenesis would be the word in English, so I don't feel the need to much here. However, just in case, the first image that comes to mind is Abraham Lincoln holding a Bible in his hand, its pages open to the Book of Genesis. Because it is yet again a feminine word, the Bible is adorned with a skirt.

4. Kitchen Entrance: Abjectement

This word is an adverb and closely related to the English word abjection, or perhaps more closely, abjectly. Whereas in English the word means that someone or something is in the condition of being utterly hopeless or miserable (which for French-speakers would be abjecte), in French abjecement has the connotation of something done in a humiliating manner.

To memorize this, I see the French critical theorist Julia Kristeva in the kitchen. She is burying Abraham Lincoln in cement, the heavy material poured over his head from an everyday blender. I use Kristeva because she famously wrote about abjection at length in one of her more well-known books.

5. Kitchen Stovetop: Abjurer

This verb means to renounce something, but it can also mean to give up on a particular task or cause. Here I imagine a tiny Abraham Lincoln on the stovetop. He is addressing a jury, a group of people growing increasingly uncomfortable from the heat of the element beneath them. Abraham Lincoln is telling them to give up their verdict and decide in favor of his cause.

6. Kitchen Sink: Ablater

This word means to remove something by cutting it, but it can also mean removing something by melting it away. In this case, I see a tiny Abraham Lincoln welding the metal in the kitchen sink. Kristeva is there again and asking him if he can do the welding later. For good measure, I have her telling him that his ablater is putting her in the state of abjectement.

7. Kitchen Counter: Aboi

Just as in English, the word "bark" can mean either the skin of a tree or the sound of a dog, aboi serves both of these purposes. To remember this word, I have Abraham Lincoln painting Pinocchio (literally a boy) over with tree bark. Off to the side, a dog barks in protest. While I'm here, I may as well add that aboiement can also be used to specifically indicate a bark or a woof, so I have the dog boxing a giant mint. The action of boxing reminds me that aboiement is a male noun.

8. Fridge: Abolir

This is the French word for "to abolish." Here I see Abraham Lincoln tearing up a copy of Shakespeare's *King Lear*. This association makes a great deal of sense to me because abolishing people is a central theme of the play.

9. Rocking Chair: Abondamment

This word can be used to indicate generosity in the sense of giving freely, but also giving material goods away to the point of extravagance. It is related to the English word abandonment in that sense, so I see Abraham Lincoln giving Pinocchio (still covered in tree bark) a huge pile of cash before abandoning him. To amplify the image, I hear Pinocchio cry out, "don't abandon me! I'm just a boy!"

By having Pinocchio proclaim that he is just a boy, I get the fringe benefit of recalling that aboi refers to tree bark.

10. Television Stand: Abouter

This word, not to be mistaken with aboutir (which means to lead or escort), refers to banging into someone while walking, or otherwise disturbing their peace. For this word, I imagine Abraham Lincoln giving Pinocchio "the boot" by kicking him into the television and back into the Disney cartoon where he belongs.

Note: I recently received a criticism from a reviewer of one of my language memorization books regarding the aggressive nature of the images I suggest. I really appreciate the feedback from my readers. I responded by explaining that I personally use violent images in a cartoonish way because it is a proven method of enhancing recall. However, people who feel sensitive in this regard should experiment with other ways of amplifying their images.

As I have repeatedly indicated, when approached like a bicycle, these techniques truly have universal application. However, everyone needs to adjust every new bike they ride in order to achieve maximum results, not to mention maximum pleasure during each and every ride. Experiment with what works for you and discard the rest – or rather saving what isn't working now in your arsenal. You never know when the material will come in handy.

Chapter 9: Example Memory Palace For The Letter C

I'll never forget my friend Kirk's apartment on Chester Road. We spent a lot of time there watching movies, listening to music and talking about the books we liked and the ideas they gave us.

In this palace, I have once again picked a specific kind of word to work on – French words that start with the letters "caf." The first thing that comes to mind to help me organize "caf" words is Franz Kafka. I find this association particularly appealing. Although Kafka wrote in German, I read him at about the same time I discovered the French writer Albert Camus, and the two share several themes between them.

As ever, I want to point out that I have charted my journey through this Memory Palace so that I never cross my path, nor do I wind up getting trapped.

1. Dining Room Table: Cafouilier

This is the perfect word to start with because Kafka often wrote about characters who get themselves "into a muddle." The word can also mean a slipup, or to experience a misfire, so I combine these ideas by having Kafka slip on a banana peel and crash into a police officer. The police officer is a real dunce, and even has the word "fool" inscribed on his badge.

2. Kitchen Counter: Cafter

Another word fitting to Kafka's writing (if you don't know what I'm talking about as I refer to Kafka's writing, please make sure to check out his writing. If you haven't much time, search the Internet for *A Little Fable*. It's only a few sentences long and will undoubtedly hook you on this writer for life).

Cafter is a verb that means to inform on someone. "Ter" is not exactly rich in associations, but the English word "inter" comes to mind, so I see Kafka with the woman in his novel, *The Trial*, whom he believes may have been telling lies about him. He is burying (interring) her in a tiny grave dug from the surface of the kitchen counter in Kirk's apartment on Chester Road.

3. Fridge: Cafteur

This related word indicates a telltale or someone who snitches. It is a masculine noun, and since we're working with writers here, I have Edgar Allen Poe in boxing gloves. He's punching the dirt out of the way as Kafka is burying him in the fridge. Carrying over the burying image from crafter not only helps continue the basic "ter" sound (which is slightly different here), but it also strengthens the previous entry in the Memory Palace. There does need to be some extra work done to get the proper sound in case I don't remember it naturally, but this can be done during the testing and compounding phase.

4. Kitchen Entrance: Cafard

Cafard is a masculine noun that means cockroach. If you make it coup de cafard, it can mean that you are feeling down or depressed.

As it happens, Kafka wrote *The Metamorphosis*, a novel about a young man who turns into a giant insect. In this case, I may simply elect to use some dialogue along with the image. I see Kafka in the entrance of Kirk's kitchen in the shape of a human bug. He's on his back and can't turn himself over. Because of this, he bewails the fact that life is hard.

Chapter 10: Example Memory Palace For The Letter F

I will use my friend Xavier Faucher's house for the letter F. It is especially nice to use it because his name is just about as French as they come.

As always, I have started at the back of the palace and moved forward to prevent myself from getting trapped. I also make sure that I never cross my path in order to avoid confusing myself.

Finally, to speed my progress in learning, I pick a particular kind of F word, in the case of this example, "fac" words. I do this because it allows me to pick an image that can carry across a number of different stations in the F Memory Palace.

I like the idea of using a smiley face in this Memory Palace because Xavier Faucher is not particularly prone to expressing his happiness about anything.

1. Guest Bedroom: Facteur

Facteur is an interesting word because it can mean mailman, manufacturer or refer to a factor in math. Xavier is a philosopher by trade and uses a lot of math to generate proofs for certain concepts, so I have him dressed as a mailman. He has a huge, painfully exaggerated smile on his face as he counts out a number of envelopes with boxing gloves on his hands (it's a masculine noun) and tosses them onto the floor one by one.

2. Guest Bedroom Entrance: Factice

This word refers to things that are artificial, false or contrived. It can be a neutral term, in the sense that some art is based on imitation. In the case of an objet factice, we are referring to a dummy, Pinocchio perhaps. Factice can also have negative implications, such as when someone is a false friend or dresses something up to make it seem more beautiful than it actually is.

To remember this word, I see Xavier at this station doing a striptease with a "World Book of Facts" in his arms. He has a huge smiley face tattooed on his bicep.

3. Main Bedroom: Factoration

This word refers to an invoice, taking us back to the mathematical implications of the word facteur. I see Xavier in his mailman's uniform once again, this time writing out an invoice for services rendered. Because this word is a feminine noun, Xavier's smile looks doubly ridiculous with that skirt he's wearing.

Note: At this point, I have run out of "fac" words that I am interested in memorizing at this moment. I could now turn to "fad" (there aren't many) or some other grouping starting with F. If you are using this method, the point would be to think of another image that fits with the first few letters of the word and group them all together.

You do not have to proceed alphabetically, however. We've already mentioned grouping words together by theme. Another possibility is simply to gather random words together that happen to start with the same letter.

There is a mental exercise that I enjoy using that you might try. It involves alternating words with different beginnings within the Memory Palace for a particular letter. This creates a bit of a challenge and keeps things interesting.

For example, one could alternate between "fab" words (represented by George Harrison from the Beatles) and "fac" words (an exaggerated smiley face):

Fabulateur

Facette

Fabuler

Facteur

Fabuleusement

Factionnaire, etc.

The possibilities for creating new challenges for yourself are endless. The benefits of doing this go beyond language acquisition as well. They stimulate general brain health, which means better mental health and improved cognitive skills.

Don't be afraid to experiment with your Memory Palaces. Anything that doesn't work can be revisited, revamped, repaired or simply cleaned away. The only mistakes you can make with this form of memorization are to not use it once you've learned the technique.

Chapter 11: Choosing The Most Important Words, Building Focus And Overcoming Procrastination For The Achievement Of Fluency

I've had many students approach me and say, "This is fantastic. I've been working at this and regularly memorize over a hundred words in a day. However, what I don't really know is which words should I be focusing on in order to see the greatest improvement when it comes to fluency?"

This question is very good and very important. One of the first things a person can do is pop the phrase: "100 most important words in French" into Google. You can also search for "French word frequency." Doing this will give you plenty of lists from which to build a learning strategy.

In addition to those lists, I would like to share with you the words I have initially focused on in order to be able to understand as well as speak in the most intelligible way as quickly as possible.

First, however, let me discuss a few points about learning and concentration. A more sophisticated understanding of these concepts will make for better Memory Palace experiences.

One way of thinking about learning and memorization is to see them as two different skills. However, learning a language is essentially memorizing its words so that you can use them with ease whenever you like. Fundamentally, then, all learning is memorization and all memorization is learning. The only question lurking in between, particularly with respect to language learning, is do you have to understand what you've remembered in order to remember it.

The answer, of course, is no. Many times, I have learned a word and forgotten what it meant. As discussed in a previous chapter, this is why compounding images and rehearsal or revisiting the Memory Palaces frequently is so important.

However, there are some barriers that prevent us from taking these important steps. One of the biggest impediments is procrastination. We all procrastinate, and this is just something for the sake of sanity that we have to admit to ourselves. Since we all do it, there is really nothing to be gained from punishing ourselves or feeling bad about our procrastination. The fact of the matter is that sitting around feeling bad for doing nothing inevitably leads to more sitting around doing nothing. It makes the problem worse.

The author Tim Ferris, who made his claim to fame with books such as *The 4 Hour Workweek* and *The 4 Hour Body*, discusses a very interesting method for dealing with procrastination. He allows it to happen. He knows it is inevitable, so he plans for it. One of the best quotes I've heard from him is that we should "budget for human nature instead of trying to conquer it."

Why am I telling you this? The reason is because in order to develop a substantial vocabulary in French, you're going to need to spend some time. Although it really will take you only between 1-5 hours to build your full set of Memory Palaces, filling them with vocabulary is another matter. When learning a second language, depending on your goals, you can literally spend a lifetime still developing your Memory Palaces. Despite my own achievements, when I sit down to read a sophisticated novel in French, I need to put in some time extending my Memory Palaces and inserting new words.

The point is that we mustn't punish ourselves for skipping a few days here and there. As Ferris suggests, we will do much better over the long haul if we routinely schedule the days we miss. Intentional procrastination can even be inspirational because as you are working, you know that some vegetation-time on the couch is just waiting for you to enjoy.

Four Ways to Choose the Words You Learn

The next issue is word selection. It is important to know what kinds of words you want to memorize, particularly in the beginning. You can use four guidelines.

1. Examine the meaning of the words. This is a rather obvious point, but it is important because there are some words that you may not need to memorize right now. As well, it is important to pay attention to the grammatical function of the word. Verbs and adjectives may take more importance than nouns at particular times in your progression towards fluency. You might want to spend a month with each word type. By excluding word categories, you can actually learn a lot more, and also a lot more about the language itself and how it works.

2. Ask yourself why you want to know this particular word. Do you need the word for a meeting you are going to, or to understand a book you're reading? Have you noticed it in the French newspapers you've been reading? These are all important questions.

3. You might also ask if the word is a synonym of other words you know. You should always be interested in learning synonyms. I recommend investing in a French thesaurus. The reason you should learn as many synonyms as you can is because you can add depth and flavor to your speaking. More importantly, if the person you are talking to doesn't quite understand why you are using a particular word, if you know some synonyms, you can essentially rotate them as if they were bullets in a gun, and eventually you will hit your target.

4. Consider how the word will be used in a sentence. If you cannot immediately think of how the word would be used, then search for an example using either an online dictionary or a print one that comes with complete sentence examples. It's always worth learning words even if you don't have a feel for how to use them, but when working to overcome procrastination, you will feel that much more progress has been gained by learning words that you know you can put into practice with greater immediacy.

Inspire yourself by thinking about what you'll be able to achieve by having this new word firmly ensconced in your brain. This is a wonderful way to find motivation for learning. If you can imagine yourself being able to order a beer and compliment the waitress on her hairstyle, then you are essentially using future pleasure to stimulate action in the now. You will definitely feel very good when you notice how differently you are treated in comparison to other tourists who only learn the basics and leave it at that. People in other cultures genuinely love it when people not only learn their language, but use it on their own terms.

Words Useful For Fluency Building

Here now is a list of the words I have discovered to be the most useful for fluency building. They are listed here alphabetically for easy placement into your own Memory Palace system.

French	English	Definition
belle	beautiful	is an adjective describing something delightful to look at or describing a very attractive person. However, you can also use **le beau** to talk about the concept of beauty.
but *m*	purpose	What is the purpose of these changes? Quel est le but de ces changements?
certaine	certain	is to be absolutely certain. To know for certain is **savoir à coup sûr**. To make certain of is **s'assurer de**.
changer	change	is a transitive verb meaning to change money, change one's mind or to switch out. **Changement** is change your plans and **monnaie** is the change you have in your pocket.
chemin *m*	way	I don't know the way.
clair(e)	clear	is a clear explanation or to make clear; to understand. To remove something use **dégager**.
commun	common	joint, shared; **ordinaire** – ordinary, plain, usual; **banale** – trite, unimaginative, ordinary

comparaison	comparison	evaluation of differences. To say there is no comparison possible - **il n'y a pas de comparaison possible**
croyance	belief	is a conviction or a way of thinking. **Opinion** is your opinion about something. **Foi** is faith associated with religion. **Confiance** is confidence or trust as in a father's confidence in his son.
décision (f)	decision	choice. to make a decision **prendre une décision;** the decision to do **la décision de faire**
désir (m)	desire	wish; **désirer, vouloir** - want
développement (m)	development	development of a person, idea, institution, tradition, product
différente	different	partly or completely unlike not identical or the same; other ⇒ he always wears a different tie out of the ordinary; unusual
dispute	argument	is to argue or quarrel about where to go. To argue or debate an issue, use the word **débat**.
éducation	education	he act or process of acquiring knowledge, esp systematically during childhood and adolescence
esprit *m*	mind	**in body and mind** de corps et d'esprit

état	condition	the state of something; **condition** – circumstance such as weather or living conditions; **maladie** – disease such as a heart condition - **une maladie cardiaque**
exemple	example	a specimen or instance that is typical of the group or set of which it forms part; sample
existence	existence	**to be in existence** exister
expérience (in work) **expérience (in life)**	experience	**experience in sth** [*work*] expérience dans qch **to know by experience** savoir par expérience **to learn from experience** apprendre par expérience
fait (m)	fact	**facts and figures** les faits *mpl* et les chiffres *mpl* **the facts about sth** les éléments *mpl* de qch **to know for a fact (that)** ... savoir pertinemment que ... **despite the fact (that)** ... malgré le fait que ... **the fact remains (that)** ... toujours est-il que ...
fiction *f*	fiction	**historical fiction** fiction historique **a work of fiction** une œuvre de fiction
force *f*	force	the force of the explosion la force de l'explosion
forme *f*	form	a rare form of cancer une forme rare de cancer ⇒ I'm against hunting in any form. Je suis contre la chasse sous toutes ses formes.

gouvernement *m*	government	**to have experience of government** (*of being a minister*) avoir une expérience en tant que ministre
gratuite **libre**	free	a free brochure une brochure gratuite **admission free** entrée libre Is this seat free? Est-ce que cette place est libre?
hasard	chance	is luck or coincidence. **Occasion** and **possibilité** have to do with opportunity.
histoire *f*	history	**throughout history** à travers l'histoire **to make history** entrer dans l'histoire
importante	important	It is important to eat sensibly Il importe de manger de manière raisonnable.
loi *f*	law	It's against the law C'est contraire à la loi.
malheureuxeuse	unhappy	He was very unhappy as a child. Il était très malheureux quand il était petit.
mouvement *m*	motion	**to be in motion** 1. *[vehicle]*(= *moving*) être en marche 2. *[process]* être en route
necessaire	necessary	Are we teaching students the necessary skills? Enseignons-nous aux étudiants les compétences nécessaires?
observation *f*	observation	She has keen powers of observation. Elle a un grand sens de l'observation.
opposée	opposite	**It's in the opposite direction.** **C'est dans la direction opposée.**

parente *m/f*	relation	He's a distant relation. C'est un parent éloigné.
pensée f	thought	I've just had a thought. Je viens de penser à quelque chose.
peur *f* (*= fright*) crainte *f* (*= apprehension*) (*of something that may happen*)	fear	**to shake with fear** trembler de peur **to live without fear** vivre sans crainte **her worst fears were realized** ses pires craintes devinrent réalité **my greatest fear is that ...** ce que je redoute par-dessus tout, c'est que ... **fear of the dark** peur du noir **fear of spiders** peur des araignées **fear of heights** vertige *m* **fear of failure** peur de l'échec, crainte de l'échec **to be in fear of sth/sb** avoir peur de qch/qn, craindre qch/qn **to be in fear of one's life** craindre pour sa vie **fears are growing that ...** on craint de plus en plus que .
plaisir *m*	pleasure	**I read for pleasure.** **Je lis pour le plaisir.**
possible	possible	it is possible to do it il est possible de le faire
probablement	probably	Probably not. Probablement pas.
quantité.	amount	This is the word you would use for equal amount, i.e. equal amount of flour and sugar. If you wanted to talk about the total amount of a bill, then you would use the word **le total**.

question *f*	question	Can I ask a question? Est-ce que je peux poser une question?
raison f	reason	there's no reason to think that ... il n'y a aucune raison de penser que ...
relation, lien	connection	relationship, association. What is the connection between them? **Quel est le lien entre eux?** There's no connection between the two events. **Il n'y a aucun rapport entre les deux événements.**
responsable	responsible	The children were responsible for cleaning their own rooms. Les enfants étaient responsables du nettoyage de leur chambre
science *f*	science	the science of genetics la science de la génétique

sensation *f*	feeling	1. **a burning feeling** une sensation de brûlure **to have no feeling in sth** ⇒ After the accident he had no feeling in his legs. Après l'accident, il ne sentait plus ses jambes. 2. *[of satisfaction, jealousy, hostility]* sentiment *m* **a feeling of satisfaction** un sentiment de satisfaction **bad feeling** animosité *f* **I know the feeling** je sais ce que c'est 3. (= *opinion*) sentiment *m* **my feeling is that ...** j'estime que ... 4. (= *impression*) sentiment *m* **I have a feeling that ...** j'ai le sentiment que ..., j'ai l'impression que ... 5. (= *sensitivity*) sensibilité *f*
simple	simple	It's very simple. C'est très simple.
societe *f*	society	We live in a multi-cultural society. Nous vivons dans une société multiculturelle.
substance *f*	substance	harmful substances des substances nocives
vraie	true	vraie The film is based on a true story. Le film est tiré d'une histoire vraie.

There you have it. These words serve many purposes and you will encounter them often. If you use a dictionary to flesh out the definitions of these words, and better yet, a French thesaurus, you will quickly find yourself in command of even more essential vocabulary. Words are very interconnected, and the more you learn, the more you can learn.

Accelerate Your Learning

To accelerate your learning, watch French-language movies, listen to French-language music and read French-language books, magazines and websites. Being able to hear and read words as they are used in real-time and in actual contexts is essential. Spending as little as 15-30 minutes a day on a regular basis will accelerate your learning experience greatly.

Finally, practice with intention. Break tasks down into components. By working on small parts with regularity and focus, you will achieve more than if you try to cram large parts into your brain in irregular blasts of attention. Build your Memory Palaces first, fill them with words and then rehearse.

PART FOUR: RETENTION AND RELAXATION

Chapter 12: How To Extend Memory Retention Using Compounding Exercises & Generate Excitement For Learning French Vocabulary

This chapter will be useful for anyone memorizing French vocabulary, but especially for those who need to learn the language for purposes other than pleasure. Many professionals, particularly in the United States, learn French for business purposes or for work. Without true passion behind the enterprise, even the simple technique of using Memory Palaces can seem drab and unexciting. There is hope. This chapter will put you in control of how you approach your memorization sessions.

Generating Excitement

In one of his information products devoted to helping people optimize their mental processes, Mike Koenigs talks about speed-reading. For him, one of the best methods for reading a book quickly is to pretend that you will be interviewing the author on live television the next day. Millions of viewers will be watching, which means that you'll need to know the book very well, with both depth of understanding about the message and accuracy about the specific details of the content.

I think Koenigs' idea is brilliant and very adaptable to memorizing French vocabulary. When I am heading to events, parties or professional opportunities where I know I will need more vocabulary on hand in order to maximize the potential benefits of the occasion, I create urgency and excitement by pretending that I am going to be interviewed. I pretend that I have a book to sell that has been translated into French and know that people are only going to want to own it forever if I am able to win their hearts by speaking to them intelligently. To amp things up, I sometimes pretend that a movie deal is in the works, but only if I can convince the producer that I know enough French to consult on the screenplay and production.

There are many motivational tricks like this that you can use to get excited if you don't naturally feel motivated to learn and memorize French vocabulary.

Compounding

When revisiting your words, you will sometimes discover that you cannot perfectly recall certain words and their meanings. You feel sure that your images are vibrant, well located and buzzing with action and energy. Yet, when you look for the words, you still struggle to recall them.

This can lead to stress and anxiety because you know that without being able to call them to mind easily and effortlessly, you are going to be self-conscious about struggling when speaking or taking a test and the thought of stress alone will make you even more self-conscious.

Relax. Refuse to be frustrated or concerned because this is simply an opportunity to compound your memorizations.

Many of my students feel that they want to replace the original images they've created, but I caution against this because that can leave "fossils" that will only confuse matters later.

Instead, add to the image and enhance it. As you do, please realize that there is nothing wrong with your mind or your memory if you find weaknesses in your new 26-letter Memory Palace system. It's just a matter of compounding the images.

In addition, you might like to compound and reinforce the Memory Palaces themselves. If your memory of some of the locations you are using is not as strong as you originally thought, then you might want to work with another one. This happened to me recently when I wanted to use my old senior high school. I did my preparatory work and predetermined 20 separate stations. However, when placing new words, I found that I kept forgetting the next station.

This lack of familiarity became such a barrier that I needed, not to scrap the Memory Palace, but use it for another letter. I chose K because there are only a handful of words that begin with that letter and I could place them in a part of the Memory Palace that I definitely knew very well.

Ultimately, the amount of time you spend on rehearsing, compounding and "renovating" depends on your level of experience and general enthusiasm for memorization. Again, however, do make sure that you do your preparation and predetermination exercises as fully as possible because giving them your full attention will save you plenty of time and sweat later. When leaks in the system do occur, no stress. Simply wander through your Memory Palaces and fix them.

Chapter 13: How To Move French Vocabulary And Phrases Into Long-Term Memory Using The Simplest And Most Elegant Memory Technique In The World

The techniques you have learned thus far make it possible to memorize vast amounts of French vocabulary. You've also learned how to create a Memory Palace and use it. You, or any language student living under your roof, can now memorize French vocabulary with speed and accuracy.

The extent to which the memorized words will last depends on a lot of factors. The easiest way to explain these factors is to look at some theories and concepts of memory. Then I will teach you about "Recall Rehearsal" so that you can place any word into long-term memory. Having done this, you can rest assured that the information will be there when you need it.

With these benefits in mind, let's see what you can do to get any information you need into long-term memory.

Hermann Ebbinghaus

Hermann Ebbinghaus (1850-1909) performed many memory experiments. His findings are useful for those of us interested in practicing memory skills at the highest levels. You can find his ideas in a book called *Über das Gedächtnis*, or *Memory: A Contribution to Experimental Psychology*.

In this book, Ebbinghaus suggests that learning and retention degrade based on time and position. In other words, the order in which you learn something affects how you will keep it. Thus, the more time you spend on information, or the more "primacy" you give, the greater the chance it will enter long-term memory.

The problem is that we tend to give more primacy to the information we learn first. Ebbinghaus called this the "primacy effect." We get tired, our attention wanes and a whole host of distractions interrupt us. Even the first piece of information we've learned can prove disruptive because it may be so interesting or useful. Our interest in the initial information interrupts our ability to focus on the next piece.

Another term Ebbinghaus uses is the "serial-positioning effect." For our purposes, this term amounts to the same thing, but we'll revisit it again further along because we can "hack" it. The procedure you'll learn will enable you to work memory miracles. Using this special technique, getting French vocabulary into long-term memory will be easy.

Why is this important to memorization?

If you do not practice the information you have learned, over time you will forget it ("use it or lose it").

However, this doesn't have to be the case. Here's how:

I call this exercise "**Magnetic Memory Method Recall Rehearsal**."

When you use it, you are literally rehearsing what you've memorized as if it were a stage play.

A lot of people think of the mnemonic associative-imagery as movies, but I think this is incorrect.

Why?

Because, movies are the same every time you watch them. Only you change.

When it comes to moving through a Memory Palace, the images are never quite the same. You are using the combination of location, imagery and action to trigger recall. This lets you "restage" the image stories you've created. It is a play and it's also playful when approached in the right spirit.

Quite frankly, in my not so humble, but always Magnetic opinion, if this isn't fun, either you're doing it wrong, or mnemonics simply isn't for you. I'm sorry to sound brutal, but usually people haven't gotten the method down and that's why they struggle.

You will eliminate much effort if you've taken care of the following:

- You've created your associative-imagery correctly.
- You've placed it in well-constructed Memory Palaces.

In fact, get these two things right and everything will be elegant, easy, effective and fun. For more help, I recommend that you download my free Magnetic Memory Method Worksheets. If for some reason you cannot click that link, just type in:

http://www.magneticmemorymethod.com/free-magnetic-memory-worksheets/

With all this said, the only thing you have to do when it comes to Recall Rehearsal is to find yourself a quiet place and go through the material. Start at the beginning of your Memory Palace journey and keep going until you come to the end.

You can do this mentally, but I recommend that you have a pen and pencil. **Write everything down from your memory**. Take care that you've removed yourself from the source material. Don't have your MMM worksheets or textbook anywhere in sight so that you won't be tempted to check your accuracy until later. Your goal is to exercise and test your memory.

Only when you are finished making the journey through your Memory Palace is it time to check your accuracy. If you find any flaws in your recall, use what I call the principle of compounding.

The principle of compounding is simply going back and testing your images. This stage of Recall Rehearsal is simple. Once you've written everything out, if you've found problems, either add new material, streamline it or make it bigger, brighter and more colorful.

Then Test Yourself Again – The Rule Of Five

When you're satisfied with your accuracy, use the **Rule of Five**. This will reinforce the material for long-term memorization. The Rule of Five comes from World Memory Champion Dominic O'Brien. He suggests the following review scheme:

First review: Immediately
Second review: 24 hours later
Third review: One week later

Fourth review: One month later
Fifth review: Three months later

Personally, I think you'll benefit more by reviewing more often than this. Even so, O'Brien's basic layout is valuable and you should keep it in mind.

My Suggested Review Process:

First reviews: Immediately, one hour later, three hours later, five hours later.

Second reviews: The next morning, the next afternoon, the next evening.

Third review: Once a day for each day of the following week.

Fourth review: Once a day for a week the following month.

… and from there on in, keep reviewing at least once a month, if not more often for as long as you want to keep the information intact.

If that sounds like a lot, it isn't. Depending on the amount of material, you can rehearse vocabulary words in 15 minutes or less. Beginners will need a bit more time, but the speed and accuracy you can build by following O'Brien's or my version of the Rule of Five is fast. Dedicated practice based on an understanding of the principles is all you need.

The reason Recall Rehearsal is so much more powerful than using index cards and rote learning is this:

Instead of using the "blunt force hammer" of repetition out of the void, you are using your imagination. This strengthens not only your memory, but your creativity as well. The more you do this, the better and faster you get. Not only that, but you learn more. The more you learn, the more you can learn. This is because you'll have more stored information in your long-term memory with which to make connections.

Finally, to deal with the forgetting curve and to hack the primacy effect, do the following during Recall Rehearsal:

- Travel your Memory Palace journeys forwards
- Travel them backwards
- Travel them from the center to the beginning

- Travel them from the center to the end
- Travel them by leapfrogging forward and backwards

By taking time to do this during your Rule of Five routines, you'll ensure that the information enters your long-term memory fast.

Give these techniques a try and be sure to tell me how you do or let me know if you have any questions by emailing me at learnandmemorize@zoho.com.

Chapter 14: How to Use Relaxation For French Vocabulary Memorization

A friend of mine suggested that I call this chapter "Relax to Rememberize," but I thought it rather too cute. "Remembercize" was another suggestion – and I ultimately cannot disagree with the connotation that remembering is a kind of exercise.

Harry Lorayne has pointed out that one of the reasons why we can't remember the names of people we meet is because we haven't paid attention to them in the first place. I believe that tension, stress and not being present gets in the way of the attention needed for Memory Palace work.

The number one reason you want to be relaxed when you learn vocabulary is because it will train you to be relaxed when you are trying to recall the words in normal conversation. Nothing is worse than knowing a word, but being unable to recall it due to nervousness or feeling as if you are on the spot.

To that end, I want to share with you some principles of breathing that you can use while memorizing vocabulary. Because many of us experience confidence issues around our memories, we need relaxation in order to overcome such boundaries. Fortunately, this is easily done.

The two main strategies I use have wider applications than memory work alone. I recommend using them every day for general health as well. I know of nine breathing techniques overall, one of which I will discuss in this chapter. It is called Pendulum breathing. The second involves progressive muscle relaxation.

Pendulum Breathing

If you've ever seen a pendulum, then you know that there is an interesting moment at the end of each cycle where the pendulum seems to hang for an instant and then move a little bit more in the first direction before falling back the other way. It does this back and forth. Pendulum Breathing works much in this way.

To start with Pendulum Breathing, fill your lungs normally and then pause slightly. Instead of exhaling, breathe in a little bit more. Let the breath out naturally and pause. Instead of inhaling, exhale out a little bit more. By circulating your breath in this way, you are "swinging" the air like a pendulum. This practice will reduce stress in your overall life once you are used to doing it, but if you do nothing else, implement Pendulum Breathing in your memory work. This method of breathing makes Memory Palace construction and the generation of images and associations so much easier because you are putting yourself in a kind of oxygenated dream state.

At first, it may seem difficult to concentrate on both your breathing and doing imaginative Memory Palace building. In some ways, it is like being a drummer who is creating three or four different patterns, one for each limb. With practice, the ability will come to you. The best part is that this form of practice is incredibly relaxing.

Progressive Muscle Relaxation

Progressive Muscle Relaxation is relatively well known, and yet so few people practice it. The work is simple: sit on a chair or lie down on a bed or the floor. Next:

1) Point your toes upward and hold.
2) Point your toes towards the wall and hold.
3) Flex your calves.
4) Flex your thighs.
5) Flex your buttocks.
6) Flex your stomach muscles, lower back muscles, chest and shoulders (all core muscles).
7) Flex your hands, forearms and upper arms.
8) Flex your neck, your cheeks and the muscles surrounding your eyes.

Practice Pendulum Breathing as you do this, or at least work to conjoin the flexing movements with your breathing.

Once you have achieved a profound state of relaxation and all of your 26 Memory Palaces have been built, sit with a dictionary or a list of the specific words you wish to remember and their meanings. If isolating the terms helps you, prepare an index card for each word.

As mentioned in a previous chapter, I recommend that you keep an Excel file for the purposes of testing. To do this, without looking at your list, you will write down all of the words you have memorized and only then compare them against the original list.

Otherwise, avoid rote learning at all costs. Let your Memory Palace skills do the work. Compound your images when testing routines reveal weaknesses. Just as you would relax to remember, relax to test and relax to compound as well.

Again, realize that you want to practice relaxation during memorization so that you condition yourself to be relaxed when accessing the words later during conversations with others.

If you're nervous about speaking what you've learned and memorized in front of others, work up to it in stages. First, speak out loud to yourself. Then to a pet, (I'm serious! It's a great way to boost the muscle memory of your tongue.)

Following this gradual exposure, tell your parents or friends that you want to speak the words and phrases you've learned. Tell them that you're doing it from memory and tell them about how you've memorized the words.

Having built up your confidence, you can take your speaking practice to where it belongs: with a tandem partner, in a class and in a French-speaking country itself.

PART FIVE: CONCLUSION

Chapter 15: Frequently Asked Questions

How Do I Learn And Memorize The Gender And Articles Of French?

Many languages divide their words into masculine and feminine. Some languages also have a category for neutral words that they throw in just to torture people trying to learn the language as adults. Some people think that kids seem to pick this stuff up effortlessly, but this is nonsense. The truth is that children bumble their way into fluency through trial and error that takes thousands of hours of effort in speaking and listening as they grow up.

You have the advantage of using your adult mind to learn a language, and memorizing the gender of foreign language vocabulary at the same time you memorize the meaning and sound of a word is simple.

For example, I have set a universal rule for my Memory Palaces. Regardless of the language, I use a boxer for masculine, a skirt for feminine and fire for neutral.

I find these images very helpful because they can be instantly incorporated into all of the associative-imagery I create. No matter what, if it's a masculine noun, there's either going to be a boxer or boxing gloves involved in the image. One would think that this gets repetitive over the larger

> **Associative-imagery:**
> Mental imagery created in your imagination that lets you code and decode the sound and meaning of any foreign language word or phrase.

course of vocabulary memorization, but in fact, it doesn't. These "bridging figures" become very familiar. They are almost like TV commercials. You've seen them a thousand times before and you know exactly what they're trying to sell. This is exactly what we want when using a memorization strategy to learn and memorize foreign language vocabulary.

> **Bridging Figure:** A figure such as a celebrity or historical person used in several associative-images to help with recall along a Memory Palace journey

Other people have suggested systems such as color-coding, and you might like to experiment with that too. Masculine could be blue, feminine green and neutral yellow. The important thing is to be consistent and use a set framework that works for you. So if you use a three-tiered color schemata (for example, black, red and gold), make sure to use these colors all the time. In other words, if you'll forgive me a pun, this is one area of the Magnetic Memory Method where you can almost literally "set it and forget it."

How Do I Memorize The Sound And Meaning Of Words At The Same Time?

Memorizing the sound and meaning of words at the same time is a good practice and easy to do. If you look back at the chapters with examples, you will see that most associative-imagery is engineered deliberately to bring both sound and meaning to mind by the same stroke of imagination

For review, consider the following example to learn more about how this important principle works. While writing this book, I thought of calling one of the chapters, "Lethologica."

This obscure term refers to the inability to recall a word, or the sensation of having a word on the tip of your tongue.

To memorize the sound and the meaning of this word, I first perform a bit of etymology (recommended when memorizing words in your mother tongue).

Since the river Lethe in Greek mythology made everyone who drank from it forgetful, merely imagining a raging river with mindless people drinking its froth wins half the battle. "Lethe" brings both the sound *and* the mythological meaning of this river to my mind.

(As a bit of trivia, "leth" also appears in one of my favorite Greek words, "aletheia." The German philosopher Heidegger used it a lot, not because it means "truth" in translation, but because it means "unhiding." Thus the act of philosophy, in a Platonic sense, is the "unhiding" of truth that was always, already there).

For the second half of this word, I immediately see Thomas Aquinas bopping these mindless people drinking from the river Lethe with a copy of his *Summa Theologica*. This image triggers the "logica" in the second part of the word.

In this way, I'm doing good mnemonic work by associating the word I want to memorize with things I already know. I make them large, strange, filled with action and tremendously colorful. If I were working on a large memorization project, I would also locate this image in a carefully structured, alphabetized Memory Palace using all of the principles of the Magnetic Memory Method.

I am associating with items that already have the basic sound of the word I'm trying to remember and I'm choosing items that sound like what I want to remember.

That's a key part of the process: mentally animating objects or persons that *sound* like the word or word component you want to recall. Sticking with English, let's make things a little harder.

"Lalochezia" is swearing out loud in the vain hope that it will ease the pain of an injury like a banged knee. (Does anyone actually think that swearing is going to have an aspirin effect when they do this?)

Now, there aren't a whole lot of things that come to mind for "lalo," in terms of objects, but I do immediately get a picture of Eric Clapton singing *Layla*. In cases like these, the fact that my association ends with an "ah" sound instead of an "oh" sound doesn't particularly concern me or trip me up, but if it did, I would somehow squeeze J.Lo (i.e. Jennifer Lopez) into the image to trigger that sound.

As it happens, an acquaintance of mine in the scholarly world has the last name of "Keazor." Thus, it's convenient for me to use him and give him amnesia to bring the "zia" sound.

Of course, you could call me lucky that I know someone named Keazor to use in this way. I say it's convenient, but trust me, if you start working with mnemonics in earnest, you'll find all kinds of opportunities arising like this, almost as though your mind were rearranging the universe just to assist you in memorizing it, or better said, your mind will bring you such useful associations *Magnetically*.

Let's pretend I didn't know someone named Keazor.

I could see giant keys attacking Eric Clapton and J.Lo defending him while he sings *Layla*. Maybe she's beating off the keys with a copy of Euripides *Medea* to get the "ia" sound.

Then J.Lo gets cut, or bruised (let's make this PG13) and she starts swearing at the keys. Therein lies the meaning of the word.

As an equation, then, we could have:

Clapton performing *Layla* + J.Lo smacking a pair of raging keys with a copy of Medea, which with practice using the Magnetic Memory Method, the mind will understand as something like:

Lay ... lo ... keys ... ia.

What Do I Do When Words Have More Than One Meaning?

It would be great if one word equaled only one meaning, but in the messy world of language, sometimes that doesn't happen. I'm sure you're wondering what to do when these cases appear.

The answer is to combine meanings in the associative-imagery you've created for the primary meaning of a word. Take for example "voler." Amongst other things, this French word can mean either to fly or to steal.

The answer is simple. It involves "compounding" the imagery you create. For example, instead of just seeing a bird fly away with a vole in its beak (taking care to exaggerate the image using the principles you've learned), you could see a bird flying away with a vole stolen from a cage of winged voles. Better yet, maybe those voles have had their wings clipped so that they themselves cannot fly any more.

Some people worry that including so much imagery only leads to mental confusion in a process that already requires so many Memory Palaces based upon what seems like dozens of principles to learn.

In my experience, however, "compounding" images in order to memorize more than one meaning simply makes you better at the Magnetic Memory Method, enabling you to get better, faster and stronger the next time around.

If you're worried about not being able to recall words based on so many images and so many meanings in so many Memory Palaces, keep this important fact in mind:

We stutter our way through mother-tongue words we are mentally searching for all the time. No one notices these delays in conversation, and if they do, they tend not to care. At worst, taking time to search for and decode memorized words gives a person character. It adds a bit of theater to the conversation. It also exercises the Magnetic Memory Method, which again makes it faster overall, builds confidence, and deepens the link between the muscles in your mind and the muscles in your mouth.

Which raises an important point about using the Magnetic Memory Method to learn and memorize vocabulary in any language. My assumption is that you are also listening, reading, speaking and writing in the target language in addition to memorizing information. Without this important exposure, you can memorize all the words in the world, but still not reach fluency. Please make sure that the Magnetic Memory Method is a large part of your language learning efforts, but do not expect it to do everything.

How Do I Cement Vocabulary Into My Long-Term Memory?

Writing words out by hand is especially useful in cementing them into your mind and Memory Palaces. Plus, writing by hand every day is definitely a step you can take to be more familiar, especially if you write in your target language.

However, let's be careful here. I'm not talking about writing out words by rote. I'm talking about either writing out your raw vocabulary words for the purpose of testing (i.e. writing the word once and then looking into your Excel file to check your accuracy), or composing a letter, story or some phrases using your vocabulary.

It really doesn't matter with what level of sophistication you write. It could be a shopping list or it could be a manifesto. The important thing is to experiment with using your hand rather than typing.

At a more advanced level, you can try writing with your non-dominant hand. I've been doing this for about a year now, and although it was slow at first, I'm now quite good and getting better all the time.

This exercise has a very beneficial effect. It is sending more blood to the brain, for one thing, which means more oxygen and nutrients, but it's also making my mind access different parts of the brain. As thinking and recall skills expand, the brain builds new pathways, leading to greater speed, accuracy and ultimately improved fluency.

The level above this is to write right-to-left in both hands. This practice may seem silly, but it's actually another powerful form of exercising the mind in relation to the dexterity of the hand. I haven't gone to the next level, which is mirror writing, but I'm looking forward to adding this exercise to the Magnetic Memory Gymnasium sometime soon.

Here's what I suggest you do:

1) Using one of your Magnetic Memory Palaces, place 10 new vocabulary words.

2) Make sure you keep a record of the words using an Excel file or some other means of storage

3) Get out a piece of paper and write out your ten words with your dominant hand in the regular left-to-right fashion.
(3.5) (optional) Test your memorizations by referring back to your records.

4) Using your dominant hand again, write out the same 10 words right-to-left, or better yet, try writing at least one complete sentence using one or more of your new words. This will help avoid the drudgery and temptation of rote learning. (It's the ultimate paradox that as one of the most painful activities, we so often want to fall back on rote learning, isn't it?)

5) Using your non-dominant hand, write out your 10 words in the reverse order of the Memory Palace journey you created in normal, left-to-right fashion.

6) Using your non-dominant hand, write out a sentence or phrase using one or more new words you've learned in right-to-left fashion.

Can I Use Rhymes In My Memory Palaces?

We all learn cute rhymes as schoolchildren to help us remember various facts. What if we used this method in combination with Memory Palaces to help us learn vocabulary as well?

For example, let's say that I want to remember that the Italian word "ganascia" can mean either "jaw" or "cheek" depending on the context. To memorize the sound and the meaning of this word, I could use a rhyme: "ganascia has a jaw like a geisha." You can hear how "ganascia" is pronounced by visiting this website:

http://www.forvo.com/search/ganascia/

Notice something important here. Not only is the rhyme memorable, but it also creates an image. To make it stronger, "Geisha has a jaw like ganascia," I can add an image of Gandhi kissing a geisha to go along with the rhyme and help trigger the "ga" sound.

To make the memory even stronger, I pop this little gem into a 'G' Memory Palace into order with some other "gan" words, and yes, Gandhi works perfectly in this context as a bridging figure.

Give rhyming in connection with everything else you've been learning a try. Using these techniques together creates so many strong interconnections that you can literally bounce into a boost of fluency as if your Memory Palace network were some kind of trampoline.

What Do I Do When Learning One Language Just Isn't Enough For Me?

Some of my readers are in the process of learning a third language and wonder if they can reuse Memory Palaces for their new words. I often get questions like this:

"I wondered if the location for "a" words in one language could be used for "a" words in a different language and whether that would be beneficial or a hindrance on the retrieval of memories?"

This is a great question and there is more than one way to answer it.

At one point in my study of Memory Palace techniques, I greatly benefited from Dominic O'Brien's *Quantum Memory Power*. One of the first exercises he gives you, after helping you chart out a journey through your home, involves memorizing the ten largest oceans and placing one per room or what we call in the Magnetic Memory Method a "macro-station". This was a very long time ago, but if I really press myself, I can remember that the Atlantic Ocean was in the first room, and so forth. I can't quite catch all of them, but 50%

still come back to me. In other words, the "fossils" of the original mnemonics are still there.

Since that time, I've taken the same apartment I used for the oceans to memorize an Edgar Alan Poe poem, a certain Buddhist meditation ritual, and a whole host of words that start with the letter 'F'. The deck of cards I have memorized for magic tricks is also in that first room, sitting on the desk I had at the time, the same "pack" of cards that I had originally used to remember the Pac(k)ific ocean during the O'Brien exercise.

I personally don't find creating a "palimpsest" of mnemonics to be problematic when the subject matter is completely different. Lines from Poe don't seem to "bump" into words that start with the letter 'B,' and nothing seems to be disturbed by the nearly transparent ghosts of the O'Brien exercise.

If you do find ghosts and fossils distracting, here's a simple mental exercise:

Close your eyes and float through your predetermined Memory Palace and sweep it out. You can use a broom, a vacuum, hot soapy water and a mop or whatever your imagination brings to you. This is a powerful and meditative exercise that can really help increase the power of a Memory Palace. While you're in there, take some time to "amplify" the Memory Palace itself. We sometimes forget that having the journey bright and vibrant also offers benefits, especially when we make the Memory Palaces pleasant places that we love to visit.

Ultimately, to find out what will work for you requires individual experimentation. I personally would not try to mix 'A' words from different languages in the same Memory Palace, but can imagine there are people who would have no problem with this.

Let's think this through a little further.

Let's say that you wanted to study 5 languages at once that happen to share the basic layout of the English alphabet. I don't think it would be very difficult to come up with 5 different Memory Palaces for each letter of the alphabet on paper, but juggling them in your mind might be a different ball of memory. If I were to do this, I would look for - or allow my mind to naturally sunder some easy association between the languages in question and the Memory Palaces.

For instance, there might be a certain street in Amsterdam you know very well that would be a perfect Memory Palace for the letter

A in your Dutch studies. For French, you might use the hotel in Azille you visited during a wine tour in France. That restaurant you enjoyed in Amatrice would be the perfect beginning for your Italian 'A' Memory Palace and so forth.

The point being is that you don't want to have to think about where the Palace is located in your mind. You want to zoom there Magnetically.

On the other hand, if you were working on French, Italian and Spanish, it might be possible to use a single Memory Palace for the letter 'A'. I can imagine dividing each room or station into "channels." If you set a predetermined rule that French will allows be in "channel" one, Italian in two and Spanish in three, you have the potential benefit of strengthening what you are learning because you will be seeing the relationships between these languages in many cases.

Options, options, options -

Ultimately, I think that the most important principles are to make sure you don't cross your own path and don't trap yourself within a Palace. If you can store the vocabulary of more than one language on a station-per-station basis while still obeying these two principles, then I think it could be very successful.

Other readers who have written to me are trying to learn two languages at the same time and wonder if they can learn them simultaneously in the same Memory Palace.

Here are some ideas about how to tackle this issue.

The first thing to consider is that many languages such as English and German share dozens, if not hundreds of cognates and near-cognates. In some ways, to learn English is to learn German and vice versa.

That said, these cognates rarely sound the same, so you may not want to deal with them in the same Memory Palace. It's worth an experiment, but only you can decide. You could in fact create a Memory Palace specifically for dealing with the cognates, and if you do so, I would love to hear your results.

One thing I've had success with when juggling more than one language at a time is to try to use Memory Palaces located in the country of study. For example, certain hotel rooms and streets in

Copenhagen work great for Danish and Memory Palaces based in Amatrice in Italy works really great for Italian. Of course, we can't always visit these places so immediately in order to identify and construct new Memory Palaces, so this may or may not be a solution. However, if you can take a trip in the near future, it's a solution worth experimenting with (and England and Germany are close enough to one another to visit both in a single trip comfortably).

Here is probably the easiest thing to do. Imagine dividing each room or station in each Memory Palace into "channels." If you set a predetermined rule that English will allows be in "channel" one and German in channel two, you will not only have space along that journey for more than one word per station, but you have the potential benefit of strengthening what you are learning because you will be seeing the relationships between these languages in many cases.

Incidentally, by "channel" I am thinking of tracks, as in the tracks divided by lines on a running racetrack. You would literally "draw a line" along the floor of your journey and place the English words on one side, the German on the other. If you set the rule from the outside in the preparation and planning stage, you should have no problem managing this (i.e. German always on the left, English always on the right).

Consistency is important in order to eliminate distractions during recall and the unnecessary expenditure of energy.

Isn't Grammar More Important That Vocabulary?

Granted, grammar is important. I would never deny this.

However, when it comes to communicating, declensions, conjugations and all the rest can only happen if you know the core vocabulary. Moreover, people can only understand you if you're able to pronounce these words, or in the case of writing, spell them.

(A short story: Recently, I made a spelling error with the customs office. I had shipped several of my notebooks to myself and wrote a letter I placed in the box explaining that they shouldn't charge a toll on the notebooks because, not only had they been purchased in Germany, but they were all filled out with ideas for books I've written like this one. However, due to a homophonic spelling error, I had written that I had "felt my notebooks up," instead of "filled them out." I got my notebooks in the end without having to pay a toll, but when I saw my spelling error later, it certainly made me blush. No wonder the customs officer had looked at me as if I were a pervert receiving a box full of strange … toys.)

The point is that we often get too caught up on the grammar without having a solid enough base of vocabulary upon which to build our grammatical understanding. When we put the cart before the horse, we wind up pushing instead both the cart and the horse instead of being carried. By nature and design, the cart and the horse have been placed together to carry us. We just need to get out of the way and let them do their work.

How Can I Start Speaking If I Don't Know Enough Words?

Many people express their reluctance to engage in conversations due to a limited vocabulary. However, no matter how limited your vocabulary might be, it grows even by using those limited words you may know at the beginning. Perhaps I'm a bit mystical with this stuff, but there is Magnetic power in repetition, and the more you use what you know (as opposed to confirming what you know through some form of rote learning), the more new material clings to your knowledge base.

In addition, by using what you know, you get to see how those words work in different contexts. If you only play with them in your head, you cannot test them in actual conversation.

Speaking of actual conversation, people sometimes ask me about where exactly they can find people with whom they can speak. No matter where I happen to be, I find http://www.meetup.com/ to be an invaluable resource. Just go to that website, pop in your target language, and you'll almost certainly find one or two speaking opportunities, if not more than you can shake a stick at.

The takeaway: A limited vocabulary that goes unused is unlikely to become Magnetic. Using vocabulary attracts new vocabulary. Always.

What If I Make Mistakes?

The short answer: Good. Make as many as you can.

The long answer: Mistakes are absolutely central to learning. Mistakes are the means by which we gauge our progress.

There was once a marketing genius who pointed out that he never earned a dime from his successes. All of his profits came from his mistakes.

What he meant was that success only comes from trying things out and figuring out what doesn't work. You learn more about what *does* work from hitting a brick wall and needing to reconfigure your approach than you do by drawing a full house every time.

The takeaway: cherish the mistakes you make during the memorization process, the testing process and the recall process. They will not only grant you greater familiarity with the words you are trying to learn, but teach you more about the memorization process itself. You'll be continually more successful in the future merely by paying attention to what hasn't worked in the past - though as a caveat, do take care not to rule out what hasn't worked before as eternally useless. Tides change, and an older concept may bring you good fortune in the future.

How Do I Find New Words That Will Make Me Feel Like Myself In A New Language?

One of the first things I suggest that people do is record their conversations over the course of a single day and then listen to them. Spend a bit of time writing down the most essential words that you think you would need in your foreign language.

I'm talking about words with substance, the kind of words and phrases that you could use in a pinch, even with bad grammar, and still get your point across.

Words and phrases that no travel guide will ever teach you.

"Behind the scenes," for instance, is a phrase I constantly find myself using in English. I hear it all the time also. I wrote it down and asked different native speakers in different languages how this idea is expressed.

"Unauthorized" is another one, along with "forbidden," "hidden," "scandal," "illegal" and "off--limits."

I call these kinds of words "theme" words. They're not exactly synonyms and you wouldn't necessary find them stacked together in a thesaurus, but they still hang together.

Anyhow, I plucked all of those out of a conversation I recorded that I had over Skype with a friend.

(Now, don't think I was holding a criminal conversation or anything -- we were talking about Georgio Agamban's concept of the state of exception. Philosophy stuff about corrupt governments, etc.)

Yes, it's a bit boring to listen to myself, but here's the thing: when I talk in a foreign language, I want to be myself.

If I'm talking using words from a travel guide or Pimsleur, I sound worse than an infant (no insult to infants intended -- they tend, in fact, to be far more sophisticated that people starting off in a new language, largely because they're fearless about playing around. It's the adults who are too dainty to jump into the sandbox of language and make mud pies).

It's for this reason why I think we all really need to listen to ourselves in order to make steps toward fluency in another language.

You've studied your own conversational style and made a list. Guess what you do next?

Take that list of words and stick 'em in your Memory Palaces.

Another fun way to pick up words that are important is to seek out dictionaries written for children in our dream target languages.

The benefit of doing this is not only that we'll quickly gather up the "simple" words, but also we'll quickly be able to read the dictionary definitions within the target language itself (a top priority, in my not-so-humble, but always Magnetic opinion).

Some other ideas include:

1) Study the background of the language. If you're studying French, why not get some books on France, Quebec and other parts of the world where this language is spoken? Try to get an idea of how that particular language is related to cultural customs, political structures and the general pulse of the people.

You could also head to the library and find some scholarly books about the history of the language itself. I do not recommend that you read books about grammar unless you are going to read them within the target language itself. That is something that you can start with at any time. Otherwise, if you are sitting seriously with a dictionary and memorizing grammar using the Magnetic Memory Method, then you are going to pick up more than enough grammar from the sentence fragments in your dictionary (or your online dictionary).

2) The next thing to do is read within the language itself. This could be children's books - though please don't make the mistake that these will necessarily be simple. Books for children in your target language could be biting off more than you can chew if you're just starting out, and they often feature a surprising number of words that you won't find in a standard dictionary. With that said, the pictures could be very helpful.

More useful are newspapers and magazines in your target language. If you can quickly find out what's going on using the New York Times and then glance through the same or similar stories in a major newspaper in your target language, you'll find many new words you can add to your vocabulary, and you'll discover them while understanding the context in which they have been used.

Ultimately, only you can decide which reading materials are most appropriate for you. The trick is to be interested in whatever you choose to read. If you are a person who is uninterested in the latest tragedies around the globe for whatever reason, then reading a newspaper may not be the best thing for you.

One thing that has been tremendously helpful to me involves reading books in a target language that I already know very well in English. George Orwell's *1984*, for instance, is very easy to read in German, not just because I've used the novel to help build my vocabulary, but also because I'm keenly interested in the story. It's the kind of novel that I can read once a year and never tire of it.

Now in this case, I'm talking about reading an English-language book in one of my target languages. You can also do this the other way around. For instance, I'm also very familiar with the English translations of Franz Kafka's writings, so I can readily absorb myself in his German.

Reading doesn't have to be limited to books either. For example, I love watching Shakespeare movies with the German "untertiteln" (subtitles) turned on. I sometimes watch half the movie with the English sound turned on and then the other half with the sound switched off so that I have nothing more than the images and the German text to which I can refer.

This is again and English-to-target language procedure, but one can just as readily seek out movies in the target language that feature closed captioning. This will give you subtitles of the words that the actors are actually speaking. Have a pen and pencil handy to jot down some of the vocabulary you want to store in your Memory Palaces, and you're set like Chet, as the Hardy Boys used to say.

Why is reading important? It's because you're encountering the words in context. I will always advocate raw time spent with siphoning the dictionary directly into your Memory Palaces, but this needs to be supplemented with reading of one form or another. The whole point of building a massive vocabulary is being able to encounter all of those words in context. Make sure that either you spend time reading from books or in collaboration with movies in the manner I have suggested.

It's really important to test your accuracy, or at least verify that you've generally understood what you're reading. The best way to do this is to use novels rather than newspapers. Some online newspapers, however, do come with translations in English, so that can be helpful for the purposes of verification, but these can take some digging to find.

It's easier to just identify a novel you love and then find a translation of that novel in your target language.

Here's a good procedure to follow:

- Read a chapter of the novel you are familiar with in the target language.
- Write down a list of words you don't know, limiting yourself to about 3 per page to avoid overwhelm.
- Take the number of words that is right for you and predetermine them by noticing which letters they begin with and thinking about word parts. Decide which Memory Palaces you will put them in and along with what part of the journey you have already identified using the Magnetic Memory worksheets.
- Get out your preferred dictionary.
- Starting with the first word, learn its meaning and then create some associations that you can use to effectively recall the

meaning and sound of the word the next time you want to use it, or the next time you hear it or read it.

After completing these steps, go back, read the chapter again, and notice how your understanding of the story has expanded. This should be a thrilling feeling that will inspire you to do more.

Now comes the verification procedure: Look at the same chapter in English and see how well you've done. Obviously, there are no word-for-word translations, and I don't mean to suggest that you can have 100% verification. The point here is to simply focus your attention on the meanings of the words, and how they are used by jogging your memory of the way things played out in this favorite book.

If an entire chapter proves to be too much, just work on a single page. If a single page is too much, work on a paragraph.

Failing that, work on a single sentence, but take care that you don't "undertrain." You don't want to be doing Mr. Bean-sized pushups against the wall when your body is capable of raising itself up from the floor 50 times or more with a touch of training.

For those of you who want to go further with this technique, see if you can't find an audiobook of one of your favorite novels in the target language and then read the physical book as you're listening. There will sometimes be slight variations in the text, but these shouldn't be bothersome so long as the audio production is unexpurgated.

You can usually figure this out by how long the recording is (i.e. a 2-hour recording of a 500 page novel is most certainly expurgated, but if it's 20 hours long, you should be on the right track).

Chapter 16: This Magnetic Conclusion Is Just the Beginning

There is much French to learn and memorize as you continue your adventures with the Magnetic Memory Method.

Because a solid understanding of how Memory Palaces work is critical to your success, let's conclude with some intensive review. We'll also expand on some of the most important Memory Palace concepts as we go through what you've learned.

The first step is to create a journey, but not just any old journey if you're using the Magnetic Memory Method. Instead of simply creating a helter-skelter path throughout the building you are using, obey these four principles to create effective Memory Palace journeys that will be fun to use:

- Don't trap yourself
- Don't cross your own path
- Peer versus enter
- Select your "stations" with care

Let's review each of these principles in detail.

1) Don't Trap Yourself

Over the years, I have found that many people I've worked with wind up trapping themselves in their Memory Palaces. This is because they start anywhere in their home at random instead of thinking the journey through.

For example, I'm presently writing in the kitchen. In this home, the kitchen would not be an appropriate starting point in this Memory Palace. This is because in order to have more than two or three stops along my journey, I would have to move deeper into the Memory Palace.

On the contrary, we want to move outward, towards an exit. This is so that we can get outside and add new stations or stopping points along the journey at any point we wish.

We always want to be able to add more stations.

Although a subtle point for true Memory Palace aficionados, we also want to avoid "Memory Palace Claustrophobia." This condition describes the feeling that there isn't enough space for the images we have created and left at a particular station.

I would be saying this tongue in cheek, but I have actually heard from one of my readers that this is a problem for her and I believe it! Anything that causes you to concentrate on matters other than the information you've stored in your Memory Palaces needs to be avoided. Not trapping yourself along any point of the journey is a good place to start.

2) Don't Cross Your Own Path

This point is strongly related to the point about not trapping yourself. If you have a computer nearby, I discuss this at length in a free video on YouTube I created to help a reader who sent me a map of one of his Memory Palaces:

http://www.youtube.com/watch?v=IQ6j5d7Dvgo

(If you're reading the print edition, or listening to the audio edition of this book and don't feel like typing this address, just search for "Metivier YouTube avoid Memory Palace confusion" and it should pop up).

On the map, this reader shows how in order to move through his house, he felt he had to cross his own path. However, as you'll see based on the drawing he supplied, we found a solution together.

You can easily follow these two principles by creating your first Memory Palace station in a "terminal location." This term indicates the innermost room in your home that you can move outward from throughout the dwelling towards a door leading outside. Main bedrooms situated in the back corner of a home usually fit this description. In the first home in which I created a Memory Palace, my office was the terminal location.

The path I created was as follows:

My office
Laundry room
Bathroom
Bedroom
Wife's office
Living room
Hallway
Kitchen

As you can see, it was possible for me to mentally move through the Memory Palace in a linear line without crossing my own path or trapping myself. I also did not need to pass through walls like a ghost, nor did I simply jump through the itchen window out onto the street.

We avoid movements like this because such actions require mental energy. Unnatural elements create "blips" in your journeys. You will not want to deal with interruptions like these when you use your Memory Palaces later to recall information. Keep the journeys simple, linear and based on what you would do in reality.

I should point out that you don't have to follow my advice here. I'm making this recommendation based on years of experience of my own and countless interactions with readers of my books. They confirm that passing through walls is the equivalent of crossing your own path because it distracts from the primary goal, which is finding information you've memorized.

Yet, it is important to experiment on your own. It is impossible to rule out that such unnatural strategies won't work for some people. I am providing tried and tested guidelines, but ultimately each person needs to adapt the principles to their own use. If in doubt, move through your Memory Palaces in the same way you would if you were to walk through them along a linear path along which you do not cross your own tracks.

3) Peer Versus Enter
Of course, if you're moving from room to room, how on earth do you avoid not crossing your own path, especially if you want to

use multiple places inside of each room to store memorized information?

The problem is easily solved. Instead of entering any room, simply imagine that you are peering into it. If you identify and create multiple micro-stations within the room, instead of walking from station to station, simply cast your eyes (in your imagination) around the room. There should be no need to enter it.

The important point is that you want to make sure that you circle the room clockwise or counter-clockwise depending on the linear progression of the rest of your journey.

4) Select Your "Stations" With Care

Instead of calling each location within a Memory Palace "loci" (Memory Palaces are already locations), I call these stops along the journey "stations." These stops literally are stations where you leave the information you've encoded using the other strategies discussed in this book.

There are at least three kinds of stations and a person using the Magnetic Memory Method could certainly identify more. These are:

- Macro-stations
- Micro-stations
- Virtual stations

A macro station is an entire room. If you use your bedroom to store one piece of information, then that is technically a macro-station. However, if you use the dresser, the windowsill, the left bedside table, the bed, the right bedside table, the closet and then the bookshelf before exiting the room, then these are all micro-stations within the room and the room itself no longer technically qualifies as a station at all. It's simply part of the route where you pause and peer in the door to take a journey with the eyes in your mind around the room.

Here's A Full Review Of How To Get Started Building Your First Memory Palace:

1) Identify a location with which you are deeply familiar. At this point, you should use a building to which you currently hold some connection. Again, it doesn't have to be your home. It could be your office or your school. However, avoid things like large campuses. Use a relatively contained structure with a number of rooms connected by hallways and/or staircases.

2) Find 10 "stations" within the location, which is now officially a Memory Palace in your mind. You will use these stations as "drop-off" points for the information you want to memorize. A station can be an entire room or just part of a room.

I recommend starting with entire rooms at the beginning. However, if you feel ready to "peer" into rooms by giving them multiple stations, do so. You will learn about your thresholds and limits as you explore the Magnetic Memory Method. As you explore, your mental abilities will extend.

3) It helps to draw out the floor plan of the Memory Palace on blank paper or graph paper. Again, visit:

http://www.youtube.com/watch?v=IQ6j5d7Dvgo

or search for "Metivier YouTube Memory Palace confusion" and you'll find a video depicting exactly how one of my readers has drawn out his Memory Palace and how to troubleshoot a small problem he had.

As an alternative to drawing out your Memory Palaces, you can also create a top-down Excel file. I usually do both, but it depends on the purpose for which the Memory Palace is intended.

To see an example of how you can use an Excel file to keep record of what you've done in a Memory Palace (including the Memory Palace itself), visit:

http://www.youtube.com/watch?v=UMPMuOyfke4

(or search Google using the keywords "Metivier YouTube Excel file Memory Palace).

Whether you draw or use an Excel file (or both), number each station in the Memory Palace in sequential order. Ensure that your journey starts in a terminal location (i.e. you've eliminated the possibility of trapping yourself within the Memory Palace). In addition, make sure that your journey moves in a linear line without crossing your own path.

4) Do all of these activities in a state of relaxation. Revisit the chapter in this book on the role of relaxation in imaginative Memory Palace work (i.e. play) if needed.

5) Test your Memory Palaces. Mentally wander through them and make sure that you can move from station to station without spending undue focus on the journey. The journey should be natural and closely resemble how you would move from station to station if you were really going to walk through the building.

6) Amplify your Memory Palaces. This means that you take a small amount of time to concentrate on your journey to make sure that it is vivid in your mind. A lot of people skip this step, assuming that because they are so familiar with the locations upon which they base their Memory Palaces that this isn't important. In many cases, this is true.

However, personal experimentation and the feedback I've received from those experiencing monumental success from the Magnetic Memory Method demonstrates that taking just a few seconds to mentally walk through the Memory Palace and concentrate on the colors, the lighting and even the materials along the way greatly enhances the Magnetic "stickiness" of the Memory Palace. Personal experience will undoubtedly demonstrate that this is true for you too.

One very interesting reader and a participant in my video course, "How to Learn and Memorize the Vocabulary of Any Language," shared the experience that her Memory Palaces were intensely vivified by walking through the Memory Palace and running her hands along the walls. I've experimented with this myself and it works gangbusters. Depending on the layout of your house, you can do this with your eyes closed for extra imaginative benefit.

Once you've gone through this procedure once, you can do it again and again. Because you now understand some of the basic principles behind truly effective Memory Palaces, you can be certain that the information you store in them will be easy to access each and every time you stroll through a Memory Palace in your mind.

More On Gathering Memory Palaces

One of the many elements distinguishing the Magnetic Memory Method from other trainings is my emphasis on creating lots of Memory Palaces and then organizing them in a particular way.

The classical method of organizing multiple Memory Palaces involves a "Grand Central Station" Memory Palace. Imagine, for example, using your high school. In effect, high schools are a collection of rooms connected by corridors.

When used as a central station for your Memory Palaces, instead of mentally walking into individual classrooms, these doors would lead into different houses you've lived in, other schools you've attended, shopping malls, etc.

I know that this option works well for some people, but I've found that it confuses the majority. You have to remember, for example, which door leads to which Memory Palace, and since there are so many doors and so many Memory Palaces, people both new to the game and filled with experience can get confused.

Ultimately, there is little to be gained from this process of linking together Memory Palaces based on real locations using an invented Central Station.

Why?

As you'll recall, a fundamental rule of the Magnetic Memory Method is that we must reduce or eliminate everything that costs mental energy. When it comes to creating Memory Palace journeys and maintaining our networks of Memory Palaces, using an invented gathering place filled with a variety of doors will certainly cause confusion for many people. This problem and its solution can all be summed up in one simple phrase:

The less you have to remember,

the more you can remember

It's a paradoxical equation, but it's a fundamental premise of mnemonics that is never discussed. The architecture and principles we are building do have a learning curve, but once the Magnetic Memory Method becomes second nature, it is like a very light software code that floats in the background. Plug it up with too many invented things and then you essentially have to rebuild the Central Station every time you visit it.

The Better Method

If we're not going to use a "Grand Central Station" to connect our Memory Palaces, what other options have we? Undoubtedly, there are countless ways, but I have found that using the alphabet as a structural connector works the best.

First, the alphabet is not a building, and yet it is still a structure. It begins at A and proceeds to Z in a regular and predictable manner. If you find yourself at D, it's easy to figure out that C precedes this letter and E follows. If your mind magnetically zooms to Y, then it is not an enormous feat of mental energy to see that X and Z are its closest neighbors.

Due to the nature of how we are going to assign Memory Palaces to different letters, we will never have an issue finding them because each Memory Palace will be alphabetically labeled.

Construction begins, then, by seeking out 26 Memory Palaces, each of which begins with a unique letter of the alphabet. For example, when I first created a 26-letter Memory Palace system, I used shopping malls, my high schools, but mostly the homes of friends. I now have multiple Memory Palace systems (akin to alphabet keys on a chain that are themselves alphabetically arranged according to subject) and here is a representative example that you can use to start thinking about and generating a network of your own:

A: Aberdeen Mall
B: Brock High School
C: Clark's house
D: Dawn's house
E: Eric's house
F: Frank's apartment

G: The Garage (concert hall)
H: Heather's house
I: Ian's house
J: Jessica's house
K: Kane's house
L: Liam's house
M: Paramount movie theatre
N: Northern Face store
O: Owen's house
P: Paul's house
Q: Quinn's house
R: Ryan's house
S: Simon's house
T: Trevor's house
U: Uncle Lloyd's house
V: Valleyview High School
W: Walter's house
X: Library
Y: Yolando's house
Z: Zoltan's movie theatre

Let me offer a few notes on the choices here. Not all of these names represent exactly what they suggest. For example, Zoltan didn't own a movie theatre. He was the contracted janitor who hired me to work there from 12-5 a.m. while I was a young university student struggling to pay the bills while I took the only undergraduate course I could afford that year (thanks Zoltan!)

Likewise, "Yolando" is the nickname of a friend whose real name actually starts with an 'E.' You'll also note that "Paramount movie theatre" is used as the "M" Memory Palace.

Stretching things in this way is to be avoided, but not denied. This is because the mind will naturally bring you ideas, especially when you build your Memory Palace network in a state of relaxation. It's important not to resist unless you feel that the association is too far out of whack and that you'll have to expend energy memorizing it. As mentioned several times already in this book, unnecessary expenditures of mental energy are to be avoided at all costs.

At this point, you may be thinking that the Magnetic Memory Method is a huge investment of mental energy just to get started.

Not so. It will take you between 2-5 hours to get set up and using the full powers of your imagination to hold, maintain and use a system of Memory Palaces.

If you have any doubts about their power, I encourage you to read this article by a woman named Amanda Markham in Australia who used the Magnetic Memory Method to memorize 200 words of Arrernte in just 10 days:

http://www.magneticmemorymethod.com/amanda

What I like about Amanda's article is that she includes examples of her Excel files, which allows you to see how someone has used them to achieve a memorization miracle. Naturally, she has followed the key principles we've talked about so far, including not trapping herself within her Memory Palaces and not crossing her own path.

All of what she says applies to memorizing French vocabulary.

Where To Find Memory Palaces

We've already touched on the use of living spaces and work places for building and developing Memory Palaces. However, I'm often asked for more ideas and my answer to the question boils down to the following:

Memory Palaces are surprisingly easy to discover. Although you may not be a person like myself who has moved from city to city and moved several times within each city while attending multiple schools and working all manner of odd jobs during my younger years, I'll bet that you've lived in more than one house or apartment.

Assuming you have friends and family, you've also visited countless homes of other people. Your personal history is likely also rife with movie theatres, libraries, museums and if you can think in a structured manner about outside locations, there are also parks, forest trails and neighborhood walks at your command.

Wherever possible, it's good to take a walk around locations that you will use as Memory Palaces to amplify your memory. For example, if you can visit an old school, you won't necessarily improve your memory of the structure, but you'll make the location more vivid – and this means that it will be more Magnetic.

Now that you've learned about Memory Palaces, the next major step is to always keep one simple fact in mind: every place you visit can potentially become a new Memory Palace. You can deliberately focus on the location by paying attention to it in a completely new way, an intentional way that will make the layout even more memorable.

If revisiting locations isn't possible, you can look at old photographs, or in some cases, use Google Earth or Google Maps. In the case of public places, you can often search "blueprints" or "floor plans" and see representations of locations ranging from public libraries to shopping malls to casinos. In fact, I was given this idea by someone who wanted to use a casino he'd once visited and searched the Internet for a floor plan to help reconstitute his memory of the layout.

There are endless ways to revisit locations, and again, keep in mind that if your past happens to be limited, you can always strike out into the future by visiting new locations with a prospector's eye. There is truly no end to the Memory Palaces you can build.

Once you've compiled a list of candidate locations, I recommend filling out the Magnetic Memory Worksheets.

These can be downloaded here:

http://www.magneticmemorymethod.com/free-magnetic-memory-worksheets/

It should take you only an hour or two to complete them. When you've done so, you'll have a 26-Memory Palace network with 10 stations in each Memory Palace. Because you are following the principles of not trapping yourself and not crossing your own path in these Memory Palaces, you'll be able to add new stations to individual Memory Palaces later. If you're not using the special, Telesynoptic Memory Palace technique taught in other books I've written (this technique is actually more appropriate to memorizing poetry so please forget I mentioned them unless you're truly interested in the next level in Memory Palace technology), you can also assign more than one Memory Palace to each letter of the alphabet.

For example, you could have:

A1
A2
A3
B1

B2
B3
B4

This strategy can be especially handy when using Memory Palaces to acquire the massive amounts of French vocabulary.

The Magnetic Memory Method Is Perfectly Suited For That!

In sum, the building and development of Memory Palaces takes only a small amount of time and effort. The next step is learning how to fill the Memory Palaces you've prepared with the information you want to memorize. This could be anything, ranging from facts, lists of historical figures, foreign language grammar or names and faces.

As a final suggestion, as you are filling out the Magnetic Memory Worksheets, concentrate on the journey and make it as vivid as possible. You can literally close your eyes and pretend that you are "turning up the volume" on the Memory Palace.

You can try this in the room you are currently in, reconstructing it in your mind and then making the layout bright, vivid and pumping with energy. It should almost be as if you're casting some kind of spell or attempting to manipulate reality like Neo in *The Matrix* and manipulating reality you are.

~~~

Next time you are out for a walk, shopping or just wandering around the house, consider the hundreds of locations you can use to build and extend your Memory Palaces. The more you pay attention to your surroundings, the more material you will have to work with. As well, take every opportunity to visit places you've previously lived or gone to school. Revitalizing your familiarity with the locations you use to build your Memory Palaces is not entirely necessary, but at the very least, you should perform a mental walkthrough to ensure that you have enough material for at least the first 10 stations and ideally many more.

In addition, utilize the power of your imagination and the images it brings you. Harness the power of coincidences such as those I related in the example Memory Palaces. Use the principles discussed in this book and suit them to your own needs. Never be afraid to play around, amplify and use absurdities. Test yourself and compound. Always, always relax when doing memory work.

Spend time thinking about the kinds of words you would like to learn or need to know. Analyze how you can group different word forms together and develop your vocabulary based on the form of the language. You will see many more connections by doing this.

Speak as often as you can. Hold what an associate of mine named Joshua Smith calls "natural conversations." He talks about this in a book he wrote for ESL students called *Breaking Through to Fluency*. "Natural conversation" means taking the simple conversational patterns you learn on the recorded French trainings and memorized using your 26-letter system out into the real world and seeing how they are really used by real people. If you live in North America, there are countless ways to meet with French speakers and engage with them. Meetup.com is now available in countless cities and Craigslist is a good resource. If you cannot find possibilities online, ask at your local library. They will certainly know about your local French-speaking community and point you in the right direction.

Finally, teach others what you have learned about memorization skills. Tell them how you built your Memory Palaces, the techniques of imagery and activity and give them some examples of how you've memorized specific words. Teaching is one of the best ways to compound what you've learned and to see other possibilities you may have missed.

From this point on, you are now more than equipped to succeed with the Magnetic Memory Method. I hope that the examples and instruction throughout this book have helped you see the possibilities and options you have for creating images along dedicated Memory Palace journeys that enable you to memorize French vocabulary. If you have any questions, you can contact me at any time. My email is learnandmemorize@zoho.com and I endeavor to answer all questions normally within 24-72 hours.

I wish you a lot of fun with these techniques and great progress with your French language endeavors. I would be pleased if you contacted me to let me know how you've done and if this book has helped you. Please leave a review on Amazon so that others can learn this skill also. Remember: the more you learn, the more you can learn. The same is true with memory. The more you remember, the more you have learned. Learning a new language is a special achievement indeed.

GLOSSARY AND BONUSES

Glossary

Associative-imagery: Mental imagery created in your imagination that lets you code and decode the sound and meaning of any foreign language word or phrase.

Bridging Figure: A figure such as a celebrity or historical person used in several associative-images to help with recall along a Memory Palace journey.

Compounding: Strengthening or adding more imagery to an existing associative-image to make the target information more memorable. At an advanced level, compounding can be used to add entire phrases to words that have been permanently anchored along a Memory Palace journey.

Forgetting Curve: The idea that if you do not practice information you have learned, over time you will forget it ("use it or lose it").

Journey: The path you take through your Memory Palace.

Long-term Memory: The part of your memory system responsible for retaining information for great lengths of time

Macro-Station: A macro-station is an entire room (i.e. bedroom, kitchen, living room, or bathroom).

Magnetic Memory Method: Teaches you a systematic, 21st Century approach to memorizing foreign language vocabulary, dreams, names, music, poetry and much more in ways that are easy, elegant, effective and fun.

Memory Palace: The place you store your images and information. Usually based on a building or other structure, though not always.

Micro-Station: A micro-station is an element inside of a room (i.e. a bookcase, bed, TV set).

Mnemonics: A system or device that aids in remembering information.

Predetermination: Predetermination involves charting out the memory locations and stations in your multiple Memory Palace system *before* making any single attempt to place the words you want to memorize.

Preparation: Preparation involves relaxing the mind.

Primacy Effect: The tendency to recall items at the beginning of a series more easily than those later in the series.

Recall Rehearsal: A specific means of practicing memorized information in order to place it your long-term memory.

Serial-positioning Effect: The tendency to remember the first and last items in a series quite well, but struggle with recalling the middle items.

Short-term Memory: The part of your memory system responsible for recalling information quickly, usually for only 20-30 seconds. Also called "working memory"

Spaced-repetition: A means of repeating information in a sorted pattern. Software using this method automatically places information you tag as familiar out of frequency while making words you identify as less familiar appear more often.

Virtual Memory Palace: A Memory Palace created by the user, not based on a real, physical location.

Virtual Memory Palace Elements: Any element in a Memory Palace that does not exist in the real building. Bookcases can be invented and placed in rooms or hallways.

Word Division: The practice of dividing words into component pieces and connecting each with associative-imagery.

Ultimate Memorization Equation:
    Location = Vocabulary
    Image = Meaning/sound of the word
    Action = Meaning/sound of the word

Further Resources For Memory & Language Learning Techniques

Before reading through this list of valuable resources, please don't forget to visit http://www.magneticmemorymethod.com/free-magnetic-memory-worksheets/ for your free Alphabetical Memory Palace worksheets. These are the ultimate resource for getting success with this book.

Further Resources

There is a full list of recommended resources on my website:

http://www.magneticmemorymethod.com/resources/

For amazing interviews with language learning and other memory experts, please follow these links:

http://www.magneticmemorymethod.com/sam-gendreau-talks-about-how-to-get-addicted-to-language-learning/

http://www.magneticmemorymethod.com/luca-lampariello-on-working-memory-and-the-oceans-of-language/

http://www.magneticmemorymethod.com/timothy-moser-talks-about-memory-skills-and-productivity/

http://www.magneticmemorymethod.com/memorizing-concepts-made-easy-and-magnetic/

http://www.magneticmemorymethod.com/olly-richards-talks-about-language-tech-and-real-communication/

http://www.magneticmemorymethod.com/kerstin-hammes-talks-about-the-real-meanings-of-fluency-and-memory/

Secret Bonus #1

To thank you for reading this book, I want to give you a few special bonuses. Think of this section as one of those hidden tracks some artists put at the end of their CDs.

When I teach memory skills in a live setting, I don't have a whole lot of time to impress my students while I'm demonstrating the memory techniques discussed in this book. Let's face it: we live in a world of instant downloads. People want the skills I have to offer and they want to download them into their brains immediately.

Here's what I've come up with a routine suggested by Michael J. Lavery of http://www.wholebrainpowercoaching.com to help create that effect. Within fifteen minutes, I teach students to recite the entire alphabet backwards. It's strange that we cannot do this naturally and equally strange that we need to go to such elaborate lengths in order to train ourselves to do it, but it's worth the effort. Saying the alphabet backwards is the equivalent of skipping rope with your brain. It sends oxygen rich blood to your brain and will wake you up any time you need a kickstarter and it's healthier than coffee!

Having read this book, you already have the basis for how to accomplish this feat. There's actually two ways to do it.

How To Memorize And Recite The Alphabet Backwards

Option One: Create a 26-station Memory Palace. Place 26 objects, one per station. The only rule is that each object must start with a letter of the alphabet in reverse order, i.e. zebra, yolk, xylophone, weathervane, etc. As with all memory techniques, the process works best if you create your own words.

I use Option One in class to teach my students how to say the alphabet backwards, but I do it in a sneaky way. I never tell them that the goal is to say the alphabet backwards. I simply have them first draw a Memory Palace for themselves with 10 stations. I give them ten words. When they are sufficiently impressed with their ability to recall the first ten words (zebra, yolk, xylophone, etc.), I have them repeat the process with a second Memory Palace.

With another ten words down the hatch and everyone reciting all twenty words with ease, I ask one of the students to recite the words again, but this time saying only the first letter of each word. It rarely dawns on the person speaking what they are achieving, but within seconds, the rest of the class is stunned.

Five minutes later, the students have added six more words and everyone is reciting the alphabet backwards with ease. Try this for yourself. You'll love it!

Option Two: Create a highly memorable story. This method uses a linking system taught in many of Harry Lorayne's memory books. In this case, the story "links" one detail to the next.

Here's the story that I use to memorize the alphabet backwards:

Zebras with Yellow Xylophones ask What to a German man named VUT who is a SR (Senior) with a Question for the Post Office in Northern Minnesota, Lake Kilimanjaro where Jesus asks I (me) about the Human Growth Formula created by the Education Department of the Central Brain Administration.

Secret Bonus #2

In this bonus, I will describe to you how that I have modified the larger principles described in the previous chapter to my own purposes as part of reaching my goal of easily memorizing the French language.

Although you may not use your memory to retain poetry, the order of a deck of cards or the number of your car and seat on a train in Spain, my hope is that you'll follow my descriptions of how I put these larger principles into action and see how to apply them in your own way.

Please don't skip this bonus section. There are many important clues and ideas that you can use on your own journey towards memorizing French vocabulary. These exercises were essential to me and they will be essential to you.

Poetry And Novels

I know that we're not here to learn memory tricks, but there is little that impresses people more than the ability to whip out a heap of Shakespeare off the top of your head. I'm not talking about "To be or not to be." I'm talking about the entire soliloquy.

Poetry can be difficult to remember, especially if it is unrhymed or has an unusual rhyme structure. Take John Keats's *Ode to a Nightingale*, for example. I love the second stanza:

> *O for a draught of vintage! That hath been*
> *Cool'd a long age in the deep-delved earth*
> *Tasting of Flora and the country green.*
> *Dance, Provencal song, and sunburnt mirth!*
> *O for a beaker full of the warm South!*
> *Full of the true, the blushing Hippocrene*
> *With beaded bubbles winking at the brim*
> *And purple-stained mouth*
> *That I might drink and leave the world unseen*

And with thee fade away into the forest dim

Good stuff, no?

Now, how did I memorize it? Well, as discussed in the previous chapter I started by picking a location. As it happens, I had first encountered this poem in a classroom in Winters College at York University in Toronto where I took some of my four degrees.

I remember the room where I studied the poem and the entire building very well. So that's where I started. Remember: we use places that we know precisely because we don't have to remember them. If I know where the door is in relation to the desk where I sat, then there is no need to remember that the desk is station one and the door is station too. It just happens naturally.

So let's begin. Here is how I memorized this delightful, if sad stanza from one of Keats' most heartfelt poems.

O for a draught of vintage!

I imagined myself as large and as vibrantly as possible squeezed into the tiny desk I sat in when class was in session. I saw myself drawing the word "vintage" using dark black pencil. The pencil is enormous and digs deeply into the surface of the desk like a knife. To get more action into the scene, I imagined myself working feverishly, like a mad draftsman trying to express some unspeakable secret.

That hath been
Cool'd a long age in the deep-delved earth

By the door leading out of the classroom, I pictured a fridge, and there I saw myself digging earth out of it with a shovel. I stabbed the earth deeply with the shovel and tossed the dirt into the hall.

Tasting of Flora and the country green.

Outside in the hall, I saw myself painting the concrete wall with flowers and a green countryside. This time I was a mad painter and this time, to remember the line, I visualized myself tasting the paint.

Dance, Provencal song, and sunburnt mirth!

By the door of the next classroom down the hall, I saw myself dancing, and then kicking Ezra Pound through the bars of a prison. For reasons I won't get into, Pound is readily associated with

Provencal songs by people who majored in English. Pound also went through a period in his life where he was caged beneath the sun, and according to legend, he laughed at the guards a lot. So I saw him laughing at me as I kicked him, his face badly burnt by the sun.

O for a beaker full of the warm South!

For this one I had to bend the rules of reality. There is a third classroom in Winters College on that floor, and I simply imagined that it was a scientific laboratory. Inside, I imagined a mad scientist violently cracking an egg-shaped compass pointing south into a bubbling beaker. The smoke and boiling bubbles helped me remember that the South Keats speaks of is warm.

Full of the true, the blushing Hippocrene

For this image, I moved into the staircase at the end of the corridor. I imagined a blushing Hippopotamus with his mouth full of college degrees, his belly stuffed to the brim with them.

With beaded bubbles winking at the brim

This one was easy. In the basement of Winters College is a pub run for and by students. I just saw myself trying to bead the brim of a wine glass with a needle and some thread. Of course, everything was huge, vibrant and visualized with over-the-top action. For example, I wasn't just "trying" to push a needle into the glass, but stabbing at it frantically. The imagery is somewhat disturbing, but that's exactly the point. That's what makes it memorable.

That I might drink and leave the world unseen

Brace yourself for more grotesque violence. To remember this, I saw myself drinking from the glass and then stabbing myself in the eyes with the needle.

And with thee fade away into the forest dim

The patio outside the pub isn't exactly like a forest, but I still used it. I populated it with trees, made it dark, and envisioned myself being guided into the forest as the entire picture dimmed out, like the ending of a film.

~~~

In truth, memorizing the passage was not a great deal of work, partly because I love the poetry. Being able to pay attention to the subtleties of the language and Keats' particular spin on the world not only helps, but also creates a sense of urgency for me. I not only want to know Keats better, but I need to know his poetry better. This is what I tell myself. I manufacture excitement when I don't feel it naturally. Paradoxically, I combine this sense of excitement with deep relaxation when working. This combination of excitement and relaxation came easily to me because I just relaxed and let them come to me. In about half an hour, I was able to recite the passage with ease.

When it comes to novels, the procedure is more or less the same. Instead of memorizing individual lines, I remember important plot points and the names of characters. Character names don't necessarily have to be remembered because the novelist will use them over and over again and in many cases, we'll come to identify with the characters and remember their names naturally and without any external effort.

It helps too if you understand the shapes novels tend to take. Usually there is some kind of problem or dilemma experienced by a character who is faced by something that has happened in his or her past. The dilemma then turns into a crisis that must be dealt with, followed by a strong decision and a series of actions leading to a battle or confrontation with the antagonist. There may be a moment of self-revelation during the battle that helps the character defeat the antagonist, followed by the resolution. Obviously, not every story has this exact shape, but thinking in terms of story shape can certainly help as you work on memorizing the elements of the plot.

The important thing to keep in mind is the kind of space you use. If you are memorizing 8-10 lines of poetry, then it's possible that a single room or a small apartment with several rooms will do. I usually prefer to use one room or location for this kind of work, but if you are able to compress things in your Memory Palace, you could imagine a bookshelf in a room you are familiar with and use each individual book as either a portal to another Memory Palace or as an individual signifier of what you want to remember. It's all up to you.

When it comes to remembering the key events of a novel, make sure that you have a big enough place so that you don't run out of stations. I wouldn't want to use Winters College to remember

Tolstoy's *War and Peace*, for instance, but for something like that, Broadway in Manhattan would probably do. It's a long walk from 187 where I used to live down to the southernmost tip of Broadway, but I've done it, the streets are numbered and you can easily follow it in a sequence that's hard to miss.

If you are a film reviewer, or just want to memorize the plot points of the films you see, it may take some practice to get fast enough to create vibrant, memorable and active images and store them in unique locations in real-time, but it can be done. You can also take notes and then memorize these later when you can relax.

On that note, I must say it again: one of the key points in all of memory practice that no other memory book I've read mentions is that you need to make sure that you are relaxed. If you are feeling tense or running away from a mugger (which you might be on the stretch of Broadway that runs through Manhattan), these techniques probably won't have the desired effect.

I mention this mugging example for a reason. I was once the victim of an attempting mugging on Broadway in Harlem. I know the area quite well, but I cannot use it as part of any Memory Palace because of that experience. My heart always quickens when I think of that gun pointed at me. This touch of anxiety interferes with the memorization process immensely. Keep this point in mind when building your Memory Palaces.

Here are some action steps that you can take immediately to start practicing the memorization of poetry:

Pick a poem you actually enjoy. Although it is certainly possible to memorize material you could care less about, obviously for the purposes of practice, you want to enjoy "owning" the material in your head.

As always, make sure that you plan in advance where you are going to store the material. Make sure that you are familiar with the locations and that you've "cleaned" them out. If you've used the location before, you might run into some trouble if memories from the past are still lurking there.

Work on your memory only when you are relaxed.

Avoid falling back on rote memory attempts. They can sneak up so easily, but are not the point of the exercise. Use the techniques of location, imagery and action.

Test yourself, but in a way that doesn't involve rote learning. If you make a mistake, go back and examine the imagery you've chosen. Is it strong enough? What might you need to add in order to make it stronger?

Talk to someone about the efforts you are making. This is one of the best ways to solidify your results. If you can, teach them how to do what you are doing. Teaching is not only personally edifying, but it helps to make the world a better place. Remember, the more you can remember, the more you can remember.

Avoid using places where stressful memories might interfere with the memorization process.

Secret Bonus #3

Imagine the following scenario.

You're seated with some friends in a restaurant. You have 52 individual objects on the table. They're quite small and easily stored in your pocket. These objects can be assembled and reassembled at will. Each object has a unique set of images on the front and looks virtually identical on the back. In fact, you have to turn each one over to spot the difference between one object and another.

You have the objects out on the table because your friends have been asking you exactly how you've come to have such a powerful memory. Because you know that one of the best ways to master something is to teach it to someone else, you've decided to teach them the skills you learned in this book.

First, you want to give them a demonstration.

Imagine that you ask one of your friends to reorder the objects. They can spend as much time as they like.

Once they're done, they hand the objects to you. You turn them over one at a time, look at the fronts and then turn them back over, hiding their unique features from your line of sight for the rest of the demonstration.

When you've gotten through all 52 objects, you have the objects back to your friend. To create a bit of time delay, you recite the alphabet backwards or a new poem you've recently created.

Then, you ask your friend to look at the front of the first object.

You tell him what it is.

You proceed to the next object and then the next and the next until you've correctly named all 52.

Your friends are amazed. You feel wonderful. You are now in a position to teach.

What are the 52 unique objects you've remembered with such tremendous ease?

Yes, you've guessed it: a deck of cards.

Would you like to be able to do what I've just described? Then read on, because the techniques in this chapter involve memorizing a deck of cards. More importantly, this skill is an important step towards finessing your brain for the memorization of French vocabulary.

Admittedly, effectively memorizing a deck of cards is quite complex, at least to get started. However, do the groundwork and you'll find many more applications for the raw tools you'll need to cultivate that are applicable in numerous ways, learning French being just one of them. If nothing else, setting yourself up to be able to memorize a deck of cards quickly and efficiently will give you great exercise in the discipline needed in the Preparation and Determination department.

Think about this chapter in terms of the *Karate Kid*. Remember the way Mister Miyagi made young Daniel-san wash cars and mop the floor. There seemed to be no purpose in it, certainly not in terms of reaching his goals with karate. Yet, when the time came to actually implement karate skills, blammo, Daniel-san had them all at hand. So please don't underestimate the power of squats and pushups, which is essentially what this chapter is all about.

All that said, let me note that I also wanted to learn how to memorize the order of a randomly shuffled deck for the purposes of doing amazing magic tricks. I wound up gaining a lot more in the process, about memory, about the French language and about myself. Ultimately, there's no direct way to describe how and why this process helped me with the acquisition of French other than to say that I couldn't have figured out the path without taking each and every step of my particular journey. I also learned a lot about what doesn't work for me when it comes to memorizing things during this stage of my memory journey. That is why I am sharing these details with you.

Following the technical description of how I learned to memorize a deck of cards, I'll follow up with the example of how I use this system to memorize the seat number on my train, or anything else I might want to remember that this system can help with.

There are a number of stages in being able to memorize a deck of randomized cards quickly and effectively.

First, we need to learn a method of organizing the cards. We do this by giving each card a number. Since there are 52 cards in the deck, we need to divide them up according to suit and then give each suit a number. I'll explain the rationale behind these numbers in a moment, but for now, let's say that:

Spade = 10
Diamonds = 30
Clubs = 50
Hearts = 80

Now let me explain why we have designated these suits with these numbers. It has to do with a numerical sound system that works like this (believe it or not, remembering this simple list of sounds is really the hardest part of the job – the rest is just a technical application of the list):

1 = ta/da
2 = na
3 = ma
4 = ra
5 = la
6 = cha/ja
7 = ka
8 = fa/va
9 = ba/pa
0 = sa

I know what you must be thinking: these memory people are nuts! Well, there is some truth to that, but let's carry on with developing the technique.

Spades

Remember that we said the Spades are assigned the number 10. The reason for this will start to become clear when you look at the following:

Ace of Spades = 11 (Toad)
2 of Spades = 12 (Tin)
3 of Spades = 13 (Dam)
4 of Spades = 14 (Tire)

5 of Spades = 15 (Tail)
6 of Spades = 16 (Dish)
7 of Spades = 17 (Tack)
8 of Spades = 18 (TV)
9 of Spades = 19 (Tape)
10 of Spades = 20 (Nose)
Jack of Spades = 21 (Nut)
Queen of Spades = 22 (Nun)
King of Spades = 23 (Enemy)

Now, we start with the Ace of Spades as the number 11 simply to give the order a nicer sequence. Since the sound for 1 is "ta" or "da," I have made the word Toad as my association for the Ace of Spades. You could come up with whatever word you like based on "ta" or "da" sounds, but I would recommend that you pick something that can be easily imagined and placed into action in some way.

Just to be clear how the sequence works, I'll point out that the 2 of Spades is "Tin" in my system because the sound for 1 is "ta" (or "da") and the sound for 2 is "na." Therefore, 12, which is the 2 of Spades could be "tan," or "dan." Surely there are other options, but "tin" has always worked well for me.

Another tip that you might find useful is to pick words that have some personal meaning if you can. 3 of Spades is "dam" for me, not only because as a card associated with 13 is "dam" a logical word, but it also reminds me of when my father worked on a huge dam-building project. He brought me out there a few times, and to my childlike imagination, it was amazing to see the scope of that project. In fact, I think it would probably seem pretty amazing to anyone of any age. The point here is that the more personal the image is, the more staying power it has.

Now, assuming you have this system in place let me briefly explain why after the 9 of Spades, we switch from words that start with "t" or "d" to words that start with "n." The reason is that the 9 is represented as the 19th card in the sequence, and since 1 is "ta" and 9 is "pa," I have chosen the word "tape." The Jack of Spades, however, is the 20th card. Since 2 is a "na" sound and 0 is a "sa" sound, I have selected the word "nose."

Before I give you my personal keywords for the rest of the deck, let me give you a quick example of how I would use this system just using a single suit. Let's say that I want to remember that the 9 of Spades comes on top of the 3 of Spades in a stack I am trying to memorize. I would imagine a giant role of tape manically wrapping up a huge concrete dam. Later, when I wanted to remember which order the two cards came in, it would simply be a matter of remembering the absurd image of a roll of tape crazily unraveling over the surface of a dam, as if to secure it from cracking apart in an earthquake. In fact, in order to really make it memorable, I might want to add a detail like that. This is called "giving the association a reason." If there is a reason, no matter how absurd, that a role of tape is wrapping up a large concrete structure, then it can help with remembering it.

Diamonds

Let's carry on to see how I've portioned out the Diamonds using this system. Since the Diamonds fall under the number 30, most of this suit will start with "m" words. However, as in every suit, we eventually come to the next group of 10, which means that the 10 of diamonds will start with an 'r' word.

Ace of Diamonds = 31 (Maid)
2 of Diamonds = 32 (Man)
3 of Diamonds = 33 (Mime)
4 of Diamonds = 34 (Mare)
5 of Diamonds = 35 (Mail)
6 of Diamonds = 36 (Match)
7 of Diamonds = 37 (Muck)
8 of Diamonds = 38 (Movie)
9 of Diamonds = 39 (Map)
10 of Diamonds = 40 (Rice)
Jack of Diamonds = 41 (Rat)
Queen of Diamonds = 42 (Ran)
King of Diamonds = 43 (Ram)

Clubs:

Ace of Clubs = 51 (Lad)
2 of Clubs = 52 (Lion)
3 of Clubs = 53 (Lamb)
4 of Clubs = 54 (Lyre)
5 of Clubs = 55 (Lily)
6 of Clubs = 56 (Leash)
7 of Clubs = 57 (Lock)
8 of Clubs = 58 (Leaf)
9 of Clubs = 59 (Leap)
10 of Clubs = 60 (Cheese)
Jack of Clubs = 61 (Cheetah)
Queen of Clubs = 62 (Chain)
King of Clubs = 63 (Gym)

And Finally Hearts

Ace of Hearts = 81 (Fat)
2 of Hearts = 82 (Fan)
3 of Hearts = 83 (Foam)
4 of Hearts = 84 (Fire)
5 of Hearts = 85 (Foil)
6 of Hearts = 86 (Fish)
7 of Hearts = 87 (Fake)
8 of Hearts = 88 (Fife)
9 of Hearts = 89 (Viper)
10 of Hearts = 90 (Bus)
Jack of Hearts = 91 (Boat)
Queen of Hearts = 92 (Bone)
King of Hearts = 93 (Bomb)

These are the words I've come up with for each card using the numerical-sound system, but it's up to you to pick the words and images that work best for you.

Putting It All Together

Now, let me tell you how I put all of this together. Do you remember how I said that I sometimes have portals inside of my Memory Palaces that lead to unusual places? My memorized deck of cards is an example of this.

I have lived in two apartments in the capital of Germany, Berlin. I really liked my office in the first apartment and have used it a lot to memorize many things. In the mental version of that office as I have remembered it, there is a pack of red Bicycle playing cards (I just realized now that it may be from the cards that I got the idea of explaining to people that memory systems are just like bikes!)

Instead of playing cards inside that box, there is a garage. If you've seen Christopher Nolan's second *Batman* film, The Dark Knight, you'll know the kind of space I'm talking about. In that film, Batman's "Batcave" is actually a sophisticated room, open and bright with plenty of room for automobiles.

However, I don't have any fancy sports cars or Batmobiles in my garage (inside a card box in an office in an apartment in Berlin). Instead, I have the first four cars I owned as a teenager. I have the cars lined up in order from the first car to the fourth car (which also happened to be the last car I ever owned before turning to transit and rental cars only).

The first car is my blue Volkswagen Beetle. It was lowered to the ground and very special to me. Too bad I wrecked it.

My second car was an orange Volkswagen Beetle. There was nothing particularly special about it, but I miss it even to this day.

My third car was a silver Ford Fiesta. A bizarre choice, but I loved it.

My fourth car was a blue Chevy Malibu.

For the purposes of this Memory Palace, each car has 13 locations, which works nicely because each suit in a deck also has 13 cards.

The locations I use are:

> The front driver's side headlight
> The front passenger's side headlight
> The engine hood
> The windshield

The steering wheel
The driver seat
The passenger seat
The seat behind the driver's seat
The seat behind the passenger's seat
The inside of rear window
The outside of the rear window
The trunk
The exhaust pipe

For some people, these stations might be too closely compressed together, but this arrangement works very well for me. In general, I like my stations to be as close together as possible.

The nice thing about each car having 13 locations is that I don't feel like I have to memorize an entire deck. Instead, I only need to remember 13 cards per car. It's ultimately rather arbitrary, but it still has a psychological effect that helps the task seem less daunting.

So, taking thirteen cards, let's see what the first car might look like:

Front driver's side headlight = 3 of Clubs (Lamb)
Front passenger's side headlight = 8 of Hearts (Fife)
Engine Hood = 7 of Spades (Tack)
Windshield = 6 of Spades (Dish)
The steering wheel = 10 of Spades (Nose)
The driver seat = Ace of Clubs (Lad)
The passenger seat = Ace of Diamonds (Maid)
The seat behind the driver's seat = Jack of Spade (Nut)
The seat behind the passenger's seat = 3 of Diamonds (Mime)
The inside of rear window = 9 of Clubs (Leap)
The outside of the rear window = 10 of Diamonds (Cheese)
The trunk = 5 of Spades (Tail)
The exhaust pipe – 5 of Clubs (Lily)

Now it's just a matter of using location, imagery and activity to weave these images together. It's actually very easy and fun.

Just imagine a lamb standing in front of the car with a fife in his mouth. In addition to the horrible music the lamb is blaring from where he is not standing in front of the passenger side headlight, tacks are firing rapidly over the hood from the fife and smashing into the dish hovering over the windshield. Pieces of shrapnel from the dish have smashed into the nose on the steering wheel, which belongs to the lad sitting in the driver's seat. He winds up sneezing all over the maid sitting in the passenger's seat, and so she steals a handkerchief from Nutty Jack of Spades in the back seat who is hitting on the mime beside him. She tries to leap through the window, but crashes her head against a huge chunk of cheese and just as she is recovering, she finds herself being smashed in the face by the tail of the dog I hate, Lily.

It seems like a lot of work, and it is. However, with practice, it gets faster and easier. You'll even begin to find that you don't really need all the "training wheels" I've described as much as you did in the beginning, though they will still always be there to help you and will always remain the basic foundation of how you remember the cards. The best part is that you'll find your concentration sharpening and your attention for detail widening. It's a great mental exercise that you won't regret taking up as a habit.

In addition, it will serve as an excellent part of your goal of being able to effortlessly remember French so that you can learn the language quickly and efficiently.

A few notes on this chapter:

I do not use "ran" as a verb for the Queen of Diamonds. Here I am thinking of the Kurosawa movie Ran, which is a samurai adaptation of Shakespeare's King Lear. I actually don't picture a woman here, but the old man as he is seen sitting in ceremonial dress at the beginning of the movie.

Lily, the 5 of Clubs is not a flower, but a dog a friend of mine used to have as a pet. I never liked that dog very much, which makes it all the more effective as a memory prompt, ironically.

Leap for the 9 of Clubs is the one spot where I use a verb. I would rather not have, but I couldn't find any other image that worked for me. "Lap" would be a natural choice, but since laps don't actually exist, at least not once a person is standing, it just doesn't work for me.

As a final note to this chapter, I want to tell you a little about what didn't work for me when it came to memorizing a deck of cards. The great magician Juan Tamirez gives a number of strategies. One is to sing the order of the deck as you want to learn it. Record yourself singing the order and listen to the recording again and again. This approach is perfectly fine, so long as you want to remember a pre-arranged deck that is always pre-arranged in the memorized order. Sometimes, this is my preference, since I am adept at appearing to shuffle a deck without disturbing the order of the cards.

Nonetheless, singing the order never worked for me. It amounts to learning by rote.

Another idea Tamirez gives is to arbitrarily assign both a number and an animal to each and every card. This is getting closer to the system I ultimately landed upon, but it still leads one to use rote memorization in place of a system that lets you remember the order of the cards almost instantly.

Now that I've shared with you both what has worked for me and what hasn't, let me suggest a few …

Action Steps:

1) Make the commitment to memorize the sound system for the ten digits, 0 – 9. It's very easy.
2) Apply the number sounds to the different suits in the manner described.
3) Make a word for each card using the number system. Using a written list, Word file or Excel sheet store the words you create so that you can test your memory of them later.
4) Decide in advance where you are going to store the order of the cards you will be memorizing. Use actual locations or invent them. Since you need 52 for this exercise, it is best to think of how you can compress them into a smaller space.
5) Make sure that you are relaxed throughout this process. Training yourself to be relaxed while working on memory techniques helps with your recall. You want to "anchor" the sensation of relaxation so that you know it very well. You'll instantly fall into that state of relaxation at any time you want to with dedicated practice.
6) Get out a deck of cards, shuffle it, and begin memorizing it.

7) Test everything, but always make sure that you are not falling back on rote memory. That is not the purpose of these exercises.

8) Describe to someone else the procedures that you are using. You do not need to show off; simply explain what you are doing. Give a demonstration if you like, but focus on teaching the method whenever possible. Doing so will enhance your skills. Always make sure to demystify these memory techniques as difficult or something to be reserved for nerds, geniuses, or people who are otherwise weird. Memory skills are for everyone.

Spread The word!

Do you like this book? Has it helped you to memorize French vocabulary with tangible results? If so, I want to ask you to help me tell other people about it.

Since 2007 I've made my living entirely by writing and teaching. Yet, I have done very little promotion for my books (though this is currently changing). Nearly every sale has come from people passing on the good news through word of mouth. So now, I'm asking YOU to please help me spread the word.

Here's how you can help.

If you have an email list of friends and contacts, why not send them a message about this book and its contents?

Discuss the book on web forums and message boards.

Print out a few relevant pages and leave them in any common area where you work or meet with people. You can print your name on the copies so that people know they belong to you and use the material to start great conversations about language memorization.

If you have friends or contacts in the press or media, tell them about this book. They will definitely get a good story, article or feature out of it. I can easily be contacted by emailing:

learnandmemorize@zoho.com.

Write a review of the book and tell people where they can find it.

Post your review on Amazon.

If you write guest blogs or speak on podcasts, mention how this book has helped you.

Do you teach French as a second language or memorization skills? Maybe this book can be included as part of your course or your next product launch. You could also invite me to be a speaker and have me offer your students individualized coaching while I'm there. Contact me for details.

Thank you.

Anthony Metivier
learnandmemorize@zoho.com

Don't Forget ...

I have created **Magnetic Memory Worksheets** that go along with this book. To download the worksheets:

http://www.magneticmemorymethod.com/free-magnetic-memory-worksheets/

As a reader of this book, you'll also receive a *complimentary* subscription to the prestigious Magnetic Memory Newsletter – while it's still free. Subscribe now and get the only information that will keep your memory **Magnetic** for years to come.

Magnetic Memory Newsletter Volume 1

http://www.amazon.com/Magnetic-Memory-Mondays-Newsletter-ebook/dp/B00C4Y44K2/

- How to use dice to improve your memory.
- How to lower any hurdles that may be hindering your progress.
- Why you should try to learn each new skill you find difficult at least twice.
- How to extend your Memory Palaces to include 3000 words and more.
- How to use "Big Box" stores as Memory Palaces.
- How to memorize textbooks so you can ace exams.
- How to use video games and TV shows as Memory Palaces.
- Why perfectionism may be slowing you down.
- How to motivate yourself to memorize.
- The best time-management techniques for memorization using Memory Palaces.
- How to use free email services to memorize new vocabulary.
- What to do if you're not a particularly visual person.
- The importance of paying attention in the first place.
- How to avoid the "Memorization Kryptonite" that may be holding you back.
- And much, much more ...

Magnetic Memory Newsletter Volume 2

http://www.amazon.com/Magnetic-Memory-Mondays-Newsletter-ebook/dp/B00CMCSF38/

- How to use variety drills to improve the speed and consistency of your memory.
- The 6 negative beliefs you need to eliminate in order to achieve your memorization goals.
- Why mistakes are essential for learning and memorizing.
- Why one German professor defends memorization techniques for language-learning against the naysayers.
- How to combine the Peg System with Memory Palace journeys for maximum memorization effectiveness.
- How to create "Palimpsest" Memory Palaces for memorizing more than one language at a time.
- Why & how collaborating with a memorization partner can boost your fluency by 100%, 200%, 300% and even more.
- How to memorize new vocabulary in context.
- Where to find an exclusive - and free - online correspondence club for language learners.
- How to use to chart out and utilize larger places such as convention centers as Memory Palaces.
- How to memorize names the fast and easy way.
- Why building trust with your own memory is key to success (and precise instructions on how to do it).
- How to identify and use the "frames of fluency" as you effortlessly memorize vocabulary and terminology.
- Why there is no such thing as "memory tricks."
- Why one author claims that memorization techniques simply do not work and an assessment of his alternative approach.
- How to incorporate physical movement into your memorization procedures.

- Why the most effective memorizers always teach what they know about Memory Palaces and other mnemonic techniques.
- How to avoid Memory Palace Agoraphobia.
- How Queen Elizabeth memorized the vocabulary of 5 languages with step-by-step instructions on how you can do it too.
- How to crack the grammar code of any language using memorization techniques.
- And much, much more ...

Magnetic Memory Newsletter Volume 3

http://www.amazon.com/Magnetic-Memory-Mondays-Newsletter-ebook/dp/B00D5DYGAE/

It will show you:
- A FREE resource for finding over 15,000 phrases you can stuff into your Magnetic Memory Palaces
- How Zeno's Paradox Relates to Memorization techniques
- How to Use Super Heroes as Memory Palaces
- Why Rote Learning May in Fact Be Easier than Mnemonics
- How to Keep Dr. Forget At Bay
- How to Build Confidence When Speaking a the Vocabulary of a Second Language You've Memorized
- How to Easily Memorize Spellings
- The Right Way to Memorize By Rote (If You're Going to Insist On Using Rote Learning)
- Why Memorization Is An Act of "Unhiding"
- How to Use the Ultimate Memorization Equation
- How to Move Buildings Around in Your Memory Palace Array
- Why Spaced Repetition Software May Do You More Harm Than Good
- How to Memorize More Than One Language At Once
- How to Memorize Like Sherlock Holmes
- ... and much, much more.

Magnetic Memory Newsletter Volume 4

http://www.amazon.com/Magnetic-Memory-Mondays-Newsletter-ebook/dp/B00DQR2S36/

- How to build Memory Palaces that work like roller-coasters (i.e. automatic, thrilling and fun!)
- Why speed reading may be the ultimate enemy of memorization
- How to use the secrets of "Bibliomancy" to learn and memorize
- The power of vocalization for memorization
- How to shoot for the moon with your memorization efforts
- The key steps to memorizing systematically
- How to focus on improving your memory the right way
- Compounding your associative-imagery
- Why meditation will solve just about any memorization problem - fast!
- The most important words memorizers around the world want to store in their Memory Palaces forever
- Why having a bad memory and practicing memorization badly are not the same thing
- How memorizing a deck of cards can be used to heal patients
- The real secrets behind memorization wizardry
- The "permission-based" memorization technique that will send your memory soaring
- How to overcome learning disabilities and other imaginary barriers
- How to memorize sheet music and/or tablature
- The power of memorizing foreign language palindromes
- ... and much, much more.

Magnetic Memory Newsletter Volume 5

http://www.amazon.com/Magnetic-Memory-Mondays-Newsletter-ebook/dp/B00EAB3U2A

You'll learn:
- The truth and lies about how to memorize concepts (with practical examples).
- Why rehearsing memorized material backwards is one of the most powerful memorization techniques in the world.
- How to use TV and Movies to create effective Memory Palaces.
- The secret relationship between Batman and memory techniques.
- How to overcome the "Seven Deadly Sins" of memory.
- Why "3D" Memory Palaces betray the power of your mind.
- How to tell the future with memorization techniques.
- How to avoid the dangers of memory "charlatans".
- How to deal with personal memories that get in the way of your Memory Palace journeys.
- The best ways to read your book from the Magnetic Memory series.
- Precisely how memory techniques help fight depression.
- How to memorize foreign language cognates and conjunctions.
- How memorization multiplies your intelligence.
- How to use a GPS navigator to help improve your memory.
- 7 ways to be the MacGuyver of memorization.
- How to defeat the "willy-nilly" approach to memorization once and for all.
- And much, much more ...

About The Author

Anthony Metivier is the author of more than 12 bestselling books on memory skills and development. He has published novels, poetry, scholarly articles and is the voice behind the acclaimed Magnetic Memory Method Podcast. As a populizer of memory techniques and professional trainer, he has worked hands-on with teachers and students in over 10 countries and helped hundreds of private clients to develop masterful memory abilities.

For more than 10 years, Anthony was one of the most popular instructors at York University, Rutgers University and the University of Saarland. A former professor of Film Studies, he has worked as a story consultant on several films and series, leading him to write *Disaster Genre Secrets for Screenwriters* and *Horror Genre Secrets for Screenwriters*. The first Canadian to hold a PhD in Humanities, Anthony holds an MA in Media & Communications from the European Graduate School in Saas-Fee, Swizterland and an MA and BA in English Literature from York University in Toronto.

As a language-learning fanatic, he has studied German, French, Italian, Spanish, Arabic, Russian, Swedish, Greek, Latin and Biblical Hebrew. As a memory enthusiast, he created the Magnetic Memory Method based on the ancient principles of *ars memorativa*. By applying mnemonics to language learning in a systematic manner, he wound up touching the lives of eager learners around the world, removing the forgetfulness standing between them and achieving foreign language fluency. His "Magnetic" memory methods are easy, effective, elegant and fun.

For fun, Anthony plays Bach on the electric bass, performs miraculous card magic and lives in Berlin with a blind old cat named Baby.

You can contact him directly at:

www.magneticmemorymethod.com/contact.

Other Books By Dr. Anthony Metivier

Language Learning Books

The Ultimate Language Learning Secret

http://www.amazon.com/Ultimate-Language-Learning-Secret-Magnetic-ebook/dp/B00J1GVIAU

How To Learn And Memorize German Grammar

http://www.amazon.com/Memorize-Grammar-Specfically-Designed-Magnetic-ebook/dp/B00L9G8TO8

Memory Commentary

The Trained Memory

http://www.amazon.com/Trained-Revised-Commentary-Metivier-Magnetic-ebook/dp/B00HNYSBOS

Screenwriting Books

Horror Genre Secrets For Screenwriters

http://www.amazon.com/Horror-Genre-Secrets-For-Screenwriters-ebook/dp/B00G9I7LFY

Disaster Genre Secrets For Screenwriters

http://www.amazon.com/Disaster-Secrets-Screenwriters-Anthony-Metivier-ebook/dp/B00B0PZ5B8

Fiction

Lucas Parks And The Download Of Doom

http://www.amazon.com/Lucas-Parks-Download-Anthony-Metivier-ebook/dp/B00JD0H34Y

Last Chance!

I have created Magnetic Memory Worksheets that go along with this book. In order to receive them, go to:

http://www.magneticmemorymethod.com/free-magnetic-memory-worksheets/

As a reader of this book, you'll also receive a *complimentary* subscription to the prestigious Magnetic Memory Newsletter – while it's still free. Subscribe now and get the only information that will keep your memory **Magnetic** for years to come.

Manufactured by Amazon.ca
Bolton, ON